Often the fine shades of meaning and richness of allusion in the Bible are missed because they are based upon the manners and customs indigenous to the Near East. In this classic work, George Mackie helps you understand the background of the Bible's stories. Having lived in Palestine for many years, he acquired a great knowledge about the area and its timeless, traditional ways of life. In *Bible Manners and Customs,* he shares this insight in order to give you a deeper understanding and appreciation of God's Word. George Mackie discusses in depth the climate and landscape, native plants and animals, and the habits, occupations, mores, and folkways of the people of the Holy Land. An enduring favorite of pastors, Bible students, and laymen, *Bible Manners and Customs* will surely become a helpful, well-thumbed addition to your personal reference library.

Steven P. DuKac

1/88

BIBLE MANNERS AND CUSTOMS

FESTIVAL PROCESSION PASSING GETHSEMANE.—Ps. xlii. 4.

BIBLE MANNERS

AND

CUSTOMS

BY

REV. G. M. MACKIE, M.A.

For Twenty Years Missionary of the Church
of Scotland at Beyrout

THIRTY-ONE ILLUSTRATIONS

**Power
Books**

Fleming H. Revell Company
Old Tappan, New Jersey

AUTHORISED EDITION

8007-5179-5 (pbk)

PREFACE

An artist engaged on a classical picture and wishing to paint a Greek lyre inquired of a young university friend as to the ordinary colour of that instrument. The student had seen illustrations of its form, could quote from the Latin poets about it, and tell the familiar story of Orpheus and his lyre, but he had never pictured to himself its actual coloured appearance.

The endeavour to supply such *local colouring* to the common objects and occupations referred to in the Bible will excuse the enumeration in the following pages of many details that in themselves might seem insignificant.

It is hoped that the study of these manners and customs will convey an impression similar to that which is produced by residence in Palestine. With much that explains and confirms Scripture, the chief teaching of the Holy Land is a demonstration of something absent. The body is not the spirit and the form is not the life. These earthly accompaniments of revelation confess, by their impotent survival to-day, that they originated nothing. But in a very special manner this land has heard the voice of the Lord, and its customs and institutions still preserve echoes of the tone and teaching of the Divine Word.

Of the books that may be profitably consulted, the standard work of reference is Thomson's *Land and the*

Book. Its arrangement, agreeably to its twofold title, is that of a pilgrimage under the charge of a well-informed guide rather than a classified treatment of the different subjects. More on the lines of the present text-book are *Eastern Customs in Bible Lands* by Canon Tristram, and Dr. Trumbull's *Studies in Oriental Social Life*, both published by Hodder and Stoughton.

G. M. MACKIE.

BEYROUT, SYRIA

CONTENTS

LIST OF ILLUSTRATIONS

BIBLE MANNERS AND CUSTOMS

BIBLE MANNERS AND CUSTOMS

BIBLE MANNERS AND CUSTOMS

CHAPTER I

INTRODUCTION

He that is older than you by a day is wiser than you by a year.
Respect for Age—Syrian Proverb.

1. The Subject. **Bible Illustration** by means of present-day **Manners and Customs** in Bible Lands—such is the subject of this text-book.

In modern Palestine and Syria there are a great many things in the climate and landscape, in plant and animal life, in the habits and occupations of the people, in their modes of dress and forms of speech, that are exactly the same as those alluded to in the Bible.

This wonderful continuance of unchanged custom, during so long a period, is chiefly due to the following causes : (1) the Oriental kinship of the present inhabitants with the ancient Israelites ; (2) the close resemblance between the Hebrew language and the Arabic which is now spoken ; (3) the suitableness of the customs to the climate and industries of the land ; (4) the reluctance to admit changes under what is called the patriarchal form of government, where the sheikhs or heads of chief families, from father to son, rule over their several districts.

1

So great is this resemblance with regard to natural surroundings, dress, and occupations, with reference also to common opinion and sentiment about life, work, home, and religion, that if the same events were to happen again in Palestine, and the truths of Scripture were now to be told for the first time, the description and statement of them would inevitably take the mould and form with which we are already familiar in the Bible.

2. Its Importance.—There are three principal advantages connected with this study of Bible Manners and Customs.

(1) *It helps us to understand better the life and character of the men and women of the Bible.*—In the scientific study of plants and animals it is a recognised principle that while ultimately ministering to our needs, they, in the first instance, exist for their own. Thus, the colour and scent of flowers, the honey of the bee, the iridescence on the bird's wing, the tusk of the elephant, the "recognition marks" of the dove and deer, can only be accounted for on the principle that they are first of all useful to those they belong to; after that they are prized in the great human market, and serve us for food and clothing. Similarly, we should not grudge to those of whom we read in the Bible the first right to their own lives. They have served as encouragements and warnings to other generations, but they had actual personal lives that were lived in their own day, and were affected by the opportunities and difficulties that belonged to it. We want to speak of them, not merely as book-names, but as living people. They would not have lived for us if they had not first lived in their own generation, and for it. The more we know about their human life and its conditions, the better we shall understand what the word of God did for them and through them. One of the advantages, therefore, of this study is to impart to our reading of the Bible

that sense of reality which Shakespeare coveted when he said, appealing to the sympathy of his audience :—

> Think when we talk of horses that you see them,
> Printing their proud hoofs i' the receiving earth.

(2) *It explains and emphasises the figurative language of Scripture.*—Thus when Christ said (John xv. 5) "I am the vine, ye are the branches," and "Apart from me, ye can do nothing," He expressed in both cases the same fact of dependence ; but in the first instance a figure is used, that of the vine and its branches. Whoever would lift up this simile to see and show to others its rich clusters of spiritual truth, would do well to visit the vineyard and watch what the husbandman does in the time of ploughing, pruning, staking, picking, etc. In this way he would come nearest to the meaning that passed from the Speaker to the hearers when the words were first used.

Such figurative language is much used and appreciated by Orientals. They can employ technical and abstract terms where exactness is required, but they turn to figure when they wish to arouse thought, create interest, and carry conviction. Thus when we say "*Necessity has no law*," they say "*Hunger is an infidel*," that is, has no moral scruples. Instead of saying of any man that he has influence with his master, they say that *his hand is strong*. The most persuasive form of argument in the East is to show that something in conduct or character corresponds with something in nature. Both in Hebrew and in Arabic a proverb means a *resemblance*, and this fact of resemblance lies at the root of all Oriental wise sayings. The quotation of an appropriate proverb of this kind in a missionary address always wins for the preacher attention and confidence with regard to what he infers from it. It was this charm of resemblance, and the authority of proverbial form that Christ made use of, when He taught and

influenced the people by His wonderful parables. He
pointed to the objects in nature, the customs and occupations with which His hearers were familiar; and those
who had eyes and ears found with submission and delight
that something within was like something else in the world
without. Apart from the power of His own holiness and
love, it was an intellectual act that produced an intellectual
illuminating result. While their attention and sympathy
were given to some tale of human life and labour there
rose before them the vision of Salvation, Sainthood, and
Service. Somehow, one was like the other. As the
Bible abounds in such figurative language, it is important
that in our reading of it we should know the objects,
occasions, and customs from which it was originally drawn.

This study of Bible Antiquities will constantly show a modern
face. While we study the Oriental life in which the Lord Jesus
found the resemblances He needed, we must seek to imitate Him
by finding them in our own. Such illustrations will only flash
upon a heart full of love to Him and surrendered to His service.
Then things before unnoticed at our feet will rise up and walk in
parable; many of the common details of our own daily life will be
touched with new spiritual light, and begin to speak with other
tongues.

(3) *It explains the relationship of the Divine and
human elements in the Bible.* — This is important on
account of two mistakes. The fact that there is so much
in the Bible that is Oriental has led some to declare that
it is altogether and only human literature, and that its
claim to be the word of God is like the clothing of the
Gibeonites, professing to be far-travelled when it was
really manufactured close at hand. Others again have
regarded the human factor in the Bible as the Israelites
regarded the Canaanite in the Land of Promise, as an
element to be shunned and eliminated. This has tended
to make the Bible unreal and uninviting, and a mystery
in the hands of a special class. The truth is rather that
the word of God has always been, as it was in the days

of the wilderness - journey, a holy place and presence encircled by the comings and goings of men, and meant for them. There was indeed a centre that few could reach, but it was in the *Tabernacle of the Congregation*. It is with the Bible as it was with the Living Word, and as the Christian is commanded to be—in the world, but not of it.

As the fitly-spoken word of man must have suitable conditions of time, place, and circumstance, so it is with the word of God addressed to man. The apples of gold are placed in a dish of wrought silver. This also is of noble metal, and to make it, many threads are bent and blended together into a design, and the design is repeated to form a vessel of usefulness and beauty, but is inferior to the fruit of gold, and its purpose that of service. So the word of revelation shines in a setting of human disposition, domestic incident, social customs, and amid special surroundings of climate, country, and race.

We may take another illustration and go a step farther. The relationship of the Divine and human in the Bible is like what happens when olives are put in a new earthenware jar. Some of the oil and of the preserving salt penetrates the material of the vessel, and in turn a slight taste of the earth is noticed in the fruit. After a few seasons of continuous use the inner pores are filled with the oil of the olive, and the jar ceases to tell what it is made of. Thus the Holy Spirit was with Peter at Joppa (Acts x. 28), and with the Church at Antioch when it met to hear the first missionary report (Acts xiv. 27), but the joy over the discovery of God's purpose to save the Gentiles also was at first a shock to Jewish prejudice. The Bible shows how this taint of former associations was removed.

When the human element is recognised within its own limits, it implies at the same time a clearer recognition of that spiritual power working in and with the Bible, what-

ever our names, definitions, and theories about it, which
has already behind it a great cloud of witnesses, and still
sustains and sanctifies the children of God. In this
endeavour to know more about the people of the Bible,
to understand its spiritual language more clearly, and to
learn how God's grace was entrusted to earthen vessels,
and His power passed through human channels, it will be

JAR FOR OLIVES.

both interesting and helpful to study the climate and
conditions, the surviving habits, familiar folk-lore, and
popular proverbs of the people now living in the land.

3. Arrangement.—In exploring this field of parable
and Scripture illustration, the description will resemble
the natural features of the country, which rises from
boundary plains and valleys to central hills and mountains.
That is to say, there will be something to learn from (1)
the *Scenery*, *Climate*, and *Seasons* of Palestine; then the
humble walks of (2) *Pastoral and Agricultural* life will

invite attention ; these in turn will bring under our notice (3) the various *Trades and Professions;* we shall then pass to (4) the *Home and Family* relationships ; and, finally, from the foregoing, we shall have a general view of (5) the *Social, Political, and Religious* life of Palestine.

4. There is one important requisite without which this excursion can neither be pleasant nor profitable. An interest in the *holy life* must go along with its illustration from the *Holy Land.* It is told of the great painter, Turner, that once, when visited by two friends who had come to see his pictures, he kept them in a closely-shuttered room for a short time before he told the servant to show them upstairs to his studio. He then apologised for the apparent discourtesy, by telling them that they had to get their eyes emptied of the common outside glare before they could see the colours of his pictures. Let us seek this preparation of the shaded room in prayer and meditation upon the life of holiness.

CHAPTER II

CLIMATE, SEASONS, SCENERY, AND WEATHER

Custom is the fifth element in the universe.—Syrian Proverb.

LIFE in Palestine while it was largely affected by its industries and institutions, also stood closely related to natural conditions that were beyond the control of man, such as climate, seasons, and weather. The Arabs of to-day recognise this when they say that the Universe is composed of earth, air, fire, water,—*and custom.* As the Bible often refers to the climate and scenery of Palestine, an acquaintance with these gives interest and exactness to its meaning.

1. Climate.—Palestine is a land of sunshine and outdoor life. Although the familiar term "from Dan to Beersheba" indicates quite a small area, about the size of Wales, there is considerable variety of temperature, owing to difference of elevation; Mount Hermon, with streaks of snow in midsummer, being 9000 feet above the sea, and the Dead Sea 1292 feet below it. Yet, over all, it is characteristically a land of blue skies and sunny warmth. Snow does not fall on the plain along the coast, and there is uninterrupted sunshine from the beginning of May to the end of September. This made it possible for vast numbers to congregate at Jerusalem at the different Feasts, and for large multitudes to remain for several days with Christ in desert places.

2. Seasons.—In the circle of the year, the successive months have much the same relationship to heat and cold as in Great Britain, except that in Palestine it is always considerably warmer. The four seasons are not so distinctly marked as in more northern countries. The leading features of the year are those indicated in the promise to Noah—"seed-time and harvest, cold and heat, summer and winter" (Gen. viii. 22). The rainless period makes a natural division of five and seven months, and the Arabs usually speak of the year as summer and winter. Spring is referred to by its special name as *Growing-time*, but autumn loses some of the meaning that it has at home, owing to the fact that, while grapes, olives, and other fruits mature then, the important grain harvest is earlier in May and June. This is the time of harvest referred to in Josh. iii. 15, 1 Sam. xii. 17. In the same way, alluding to the grain harvest, the prophet follows the natural course of events when he says, "The harvest is past, the summer is ended" (Jer. viii. 20).

3. Months.—A short account of the months will show what the year brings to young and old in Palestine.

(1) *January.*—This is the month of severest cold, darkest days, and heaviest rain. Snow falls on Lebanon and highest ridges, and is preserved there until the warm weather of March and April melts it to supply the fountains for summer use.

(2) *February.*—Showers and sunshine rapidly alternate. The Arabs call it "the one-eyed"—a face dark on one side and bright on the other. They also say of it "February has no rules," and "Though February storms and blusters, it has the smell of summer in it." Almond-trees blossom, late barley is sown.

(3) *March.*—High winds, but more sunshine. The showers of March and April are "the latter rain" of Scripture, not usually affecting the deep roots of the fruit-

trees, but refreshing the standing crops of barley and wheat before they whiten to the harvest. Sometimes, however, the heaviest rainfall of the year occurs at this time. Apricot-trees join the almond in white array, like the hawthorn hedges at home.

(4) *April.*—This is the month of flowers, and the land looks more green and beautiful than at any other season of the year. Now and then hot, dry winds from the Syrian desert blow for three days at a time, melting the snow and hastening all forms of vegetation. Harvesting begins in the Jordan valley and in early parts of the sea-side plain. Fruit-trees generally—peach, pomegranate, olive, and such like—are in blossom and young foliage.

(5) *May.*—The sun increases in strength; rain ceases for about five months. Flowers disappear and grass withers. Harvesting in plains and low land. Spring fruits are ready, such as green almonds, apricots, and early plums. Vines are in blossom.

(6) *June.*—Harvesting is continued on higher ground. The land lies bare and parched for summer rest, except where there are fruit-trees, vines, and irrigated gardens for vegetables.

(7) *July.*—The increasing summer heat is tempered by cool westerly breezes. During this and the following month the peasants are busy on the threshing-floors.

(8) *August.*—The hottest month of the year, the average on the coast plain being 87° in the shade at mid-day, and considerably higher by the Sea of Galilee and in the lower Jordan valley. Grapes, figs, peaches, apples, and pears ripen.

(9) *September.*—The ordinary summer heat is often intensified by siroccos or desert winds more prolonged than those of spring, with temperature ranging from 90° to a little over 100°. Figs are dried for winter use, and grapes are made into raisins, syrup, and wine. Pome-

granates, quinces, and bananas ripen. The first shower after the long drought of summer usually falls about the end of this month, followed by a fortnight of bright, hot weather.

(10) *October.*—Conclusion of grape and fig harvest, olives are gathered, fatted sheep killed, and storage of supplies for winter use attended to. Sugar-cane and dates are ripening. Heavier showers fall—"the early rain" of Scripture. Ploughing commences, the hard, dry ground having now been softened by rain.

(11) *November.*—Continuance of ploughing and wheat and barley sowing.

(12) *December.*—Heavier rains and cooler weather. with snow on Lebanon towards the end of the month. Oranges, citrons, and lemons ripen. Vines are pruned in this and following month.

4. Day and Night.—In Palestine there is a difference of about four hours between the longest and shortest days of the year. Sunrise is a distinct moment, bringing a swift and unmistakable change over the landscape. The stars rapidly vanish, a flush of lilac spreads over the eastern sky, with long streaks of pink radiating from a yellow centre that every moment grows brighter and brighter. Then in a moment, with a suddenness that almost suggests some accompanying sound, the sun emerges from behind the hills, a glittering disc in a cloudless sky. Instantly "the shadows flee away." They hasten out of sight as if detected in evil-doing. You can see the swiftly-moving line of division between the light, with its sparkle and detail, and the shadow lying dull and indistinct. As the sun rises rapidly higher and sends shafts of light over the plains and down into the open valleys and mountain glens, you see clumps of pine, slopes of olive, and gray nestling villages suddenly springing into life as if startled out of sleep. The Bible allusions to the

approach of light and the dispersion of darkness, whether
natural or spiritual, all belong to the Oriental sunrise, and
carry an emphasis that would scarcely suggest itself in
northern lands, where the dawn, beautiful in its own
way, advances imperceptibly towards a milder radiance.
It is this authority of the sunrise, the sudden call, and
the sharp distinction between light and shade, that we
find in Is. lx. 1, 2, "Arise, shine, for thy light is come.'
See also Ps. cxxxix. 12, Is. lviii. 8, Matt. v. 14, Acts
xxvi. 18, 2 Cor. iv. 4, vi. 14, Eph. v. 8.   So the blessing
of Moses (Num. vi. 24-27) takes its form from the sunrise, and implies the same good to the soul that the sun
brings to the world.   To the Oriental mind sunlight means
Light, Life, and Purity.   Regarding purity, one of their
proverbs says, "The eye of the sun needs no veil,"
meaning that it has no sin to hide—it is absolutely pure.
These are also the leading thoughts in Ps. xix. 7, 8, where
the law of the Lord is compared to sunlight.   The same
associations give the beautiful simile of the just ruler in
2 Sam. xxiii. 4.

From 12 to 3 P.M. is the time of greatest heat,
Matt. xx. 12.   The fierce rays strike down from above,
the glare flashes up from the stony ground, the air quivers,
and the mountains have a flattened-down appearance
under the heat-haze.   Plants hang limp and drooping, birds
cease to twitter in the branches, at times the cicalas or
tree-crickets make the silence startling by a pause in
their deafening zee-zee chirping, and the shepherd gathers
his flock around him under the shelter of a walnut-tree
by the brook, or under the shadow of a rock goes to
sleep with his reed-flute in his hand.   It is an hour that
gives vividness and reality to many familiar phrases and
allusions.   To one resting in the cool shade from such
oppression, there comes a new wealth of meaning into the
words, "He restoreth my soul" (Ps. xxiii. 3), "under the

shadow of the Almighty" (Ps. xci. 1), "the sun shall not smite thee by day" (Ps. cxxi. 6), "above the brightness of the sun" (Acts xxvi. 13), "neither shall the sun light on them nor any heat" (Rev. vii. 16).

As the afternoon advances the air becomes cooler, and beautiful shades of colour take the place of dusty gray and common brown, especially where the light falls on the lofty Lebanon, the hills around Galilee, or the cliffs that rise up behind the Dead Sea.

The sun sets as rapidly as it rose. As one watches the bright descent behind the Mediterranean, the familiar words come to mind, "the sun knoweth his going down" (Ps. civ. 19). And everybody in the land knows it; not only the labourer in the open field, but also the workman down in the narrow street of the town. There is no need of city clock or factory bell to announce the hour. "Man goeth forth unto his work and to his labour until the evening" (Ps. civ. 23). When the sun sets, all work ceases.

The short time before and after sunset is the cool of the evening, when the dry wind from the land begins to blow, and quickly becomes cooler than the moist day-breeze from the sea. Isaac availed himself of it; and at Beyrout, Damascus, Sidon, and Jerusalem it is still the time when the citizens go out to walk or ride for health and pleasure.

"The beasts of the forest" (Ps. civ. 20) have now for the most part suffered the fate of the forest, but in the mountain villages, as the evening shadows move up the glens, the jackals creep out and yelp to one another and provoke the challenge of the village dogs.

Half an hour after sunset the stars begin to rush forth and sparkle in the cloudless sky. As we look up at them, with so much of the diameter of the earth between us and the light, the sky appears darker and the stars larger, softer, and more lustrous than in northern lands. They seem to stand out and reach down, as if expecting to be noticed. When Jacob at Bethel lay down to rest, footsore and weary, under the open sky, it was not strange that the Divine word of promise should gather shape and meaning from the two things that the day had forced upon his attention—the infinite dust of the earth, and the infinite glory of the stars. Travellers in the desert usually prefer to journey by night for greater coolness and safety, and still, like the Magi, take their guidance from the stars.

The moon, especially in autumn, shines with astonishing brightness, and the promise "nor the moon by night" is full of meaning in a land where it is dangerous to sleep under its rays, and where the traveller sometimes opens his sunshade to ward off the bewildering dazzle.

As Orientals reckon time by the lunar month, the day begins and ends with sunset. Thus among the Jews, Saturday night is our Friday evening, a reckoning that survives in the West in our Christmas Eve. The hour of the working-day is reckoned from sunrise; thus, taking sunrise at six, noon is the sixth hour, and the eleventh hour is an hour before sunset. The time varies so little from day to day, and brings such a decisive change as to light and darkness, that appointments made with reference to sunrise and sunset have a precision that would be impossible in a land of clouds and prolonged twilight.

5. **Atmosphere.**—As there are neither mists nor mines in Palestine the air is wonderfully clear. Travellers starting on a day's journey of twenty-five or thirty miles see their point of·destination lying distinctly in front of them, and at first wonder why they never seem to come any nearer to it. To one standing on Mount Ebal in Samaria, the southern heights around Jerusalem are visible, and northwards there is a clear view of Hermon at the southern end of Lebanon rising up behind Dan and the sources of

the Jordan. Again from Hermon one can see the plain between the Lebanon ranges narrowing towards the entrance to Hamath. From each of these mountain prospects there is a full view of the plateau east of the Jordan, and on the west, of the straight coast-line of the Mediterranean. Under this enamelling light remote objects show up clear in outline that in England would lie folded away in blue haze. Visitors to the country are apt to suppose that the land is smaller than it really is, being deceived by the clearness of the atmosphere. For the same reason the Lebanon range rising from 3000 to 10,000 feet above the sea looks less sublime than the hills of Scotland, as its appearance, at least in summer, gets no help from moist air and dark clouds shrouding the summits.

In the Bible all references to distance are in keeping with this extraordinary clearness of the air.

Abraham saw Moriah "afar off" (Gen. xxii. 4); Moses had a complete view of the land he was not to enter (Deut. xxxiv. 1, 2, 3). When John says of the new Jerusalem, " I saw no temple therein" (Rev. xxi. 22), the impression is that of one gazing upon the earthly Jerusalem where, under the beating sunshine and cloudless sky, everything stands out sparkling, particular, and unmistakable.

Thus also we have the distant recognition of Ahimaaz and Jehu. Again in the parables, the prodigal son is seen "afar off," and in the same way, beyond the great gulf, the rich man sees Abraham and Lazarus in his bosom. One of the forms of Christ's Temptation was a mountain-vision of the kingdoms of the world. In Palestine this distinctness of remote objects is too familiar to be noticed by the Oriental, and after a time even to the Western resident it becomes more real though not more beloved than the soft blue obscurities of the English horizon. The transmission of sound in the clear elastic air of these lands is also remarkable. Visitors newly arrived in Palestine are apt to think that voices in the street are speaking in the house ; proclamations are made to a whole village from the roof of the sheikh's house ; in the city the voice of the muezzin in the mosque-tower calls the neighbourhood to prayer from sleep and work, and peasants converse on opposite sides of a wide valley.

The Bible also speaks of such public announcement from the house-top (Luke xii. 3). Again, when Moses and Joshua were coming down from the Mount, the shout of battle was distinguished from the sound that floated up to them—the rhythmic beating of the idolatrous dance (Ex. xxxii. 17, 18). Similarly Saul recognises the voice of David on the distant height (1 Sam. xxvi. 13, 17), cf. Judges ix. 7. Other instances might be mentioned, such as the reading of the law at Ebal and Gerizim (Josh. viii. 33), the open-air utterances of Solomon (2 Chron. vi.) and Ezra (Neh. viii.), and generally the preaching of the Lord Jesus to large multitudes.

6. Landscape.—When Palestine is seen for the first time, the eye is charmed with the bright distinctness of everything and with the beautiful blue of sea and sky. Then comes a feeling of disappointment as favourite features of beautiful scenery in other lands are looked for in vain. There are no farm-houses dotting the landscape ; no fields of grass, no horses or cattle grazing at liberty ; no forests are visible ; the lakes lie low in the Jordan valley ; the rivers are small, and the brooks are dry in summer. Where are the cedars, vines, fig-trees, and the beauty of the olive ? Is this the Promised Land ? Was this the inheritance of the chosen people ?

Notwithstanding the deterioration that the land has undergone since the time of the kingdom of Israel and the Roman Empire, it is still beautiful when the eye has learnt what to look for. The chief glory of Palestine is in its colour, the beautiful tints of morning and evening, and the purity of its atmosphere.   There is much to enjoy and admire in the restful outline of the great Lebanon range, the sublimity of the mountain gorges, the weird desolation of the wilderness, the great olive forest of Beyrout, the green loveliness of Damascus and Nablous (Shechem), the palm-adorned plains of Acre and Jaffa, and the gorgeous sunsets on the Lake of Galilee and the Dead Sea.

Have you ever wondered why the Bible seldom describes scenery after the manner of modern travellers? Why is there not more notice of the effect of landscape-beauty on the mind, and of companionship with what we call the moods of nature?   Nature is rather a servant who has to wait and bring what is wanted, than a teacher to whom the pupils come for inspiration and beautiful ideals.   The inquiry is instructive when we remember that the Bible abounds in instances of accurate indication of artistic effect when the occasion requires it.   Thus in Ps. lxxx. the resemblance between Israel and a ruined vineyard is wrought out with much detail.   An artist reads with rapture the description of the downfall of Tyre (Ezek. xxvii.), and calls it pre-Raphaelite, bold in particulars of reality.   Again, in the Song of Songs iv. 1, dark, glossy hair is very effectively likened to the intense luminous black of a flock of goats on the hillside, and in ver. 3, the comparison of an olive brow to the smooth rind of a pome-granate, with its pale skin-like gloss and green shading for the temples, is a simile that would satisfy the fastidious eye of a Herkomer or Tennyson.   But one feels that a different range of feeling is reached when the Christian poet says :—

> And beauty born of murmuring sound
> Shall pass into her face.[1]

In one case nature remains outside, passive and appealing

[1] Wordsworth's "Teaching of Nature."

2

to the senses; in the other she has passed within, is active, and moulds the disposition.

In explanation of this three reasons may be given :—

(1) *The special purpose of the Bible.*—The Bible is the Word of God, its message is from Him, about Him, and ultimately, even in our salvation, for Him. Its first place is not for nature, but for the God of nature and of the soul. When reference is made to the sublime and beautiful in the external world, it is to proclaim that the Lord rejoices in His works and rules over all. This supreme connection is never lost although nature is sometimes represented as a personality and rejoicing in herself. (Ps. xxix., lxv., cxiv.) Thus in Ps. civ. the survey of wonderful adaptation becomes a hymn of praise to the wisdom and power of the Creator. " O Lord, how manifold are Thy works !" Compare Job xxviii., Ps. cxlvii., cxlviii., Is. lx., Hab. iii. Much in the same way, when an Oriental is shown anything beautiful or wonderful in nature he almost invariably exclaims, "Praise to the Creator !" Such absorbing pre-occupation with God's glory and the moral life explains how in the Psalms, Prophecies, Gospels, and Epistles the objects and effects of natural scenery are only referred to when serving the purposes of illustration. It is owing to this important connection with solemn and sacred subjects, that natural objects in Palestine, the humble implements of its trades, and the various parts and furnishings of its houses, have a sanctity and symbolism unmet with elsewhere. It is almost with a feeling of profanation that the Western resident watches the people of Palestine in their ordinary work doing things that to us, but not usually to them, wear a high meaning of parable, and handling with simple unconcern things that to us have become exponents of the Gospel and preachers of immortality.

Thus the Lebanon peasant stands on the threshing-floor

with his fan or wooden pitchfork in his hand, and separates
the wheat from the chaff. Peasants come to the Jordan
ford and wade waist-deep across the stream, and one stands
mid-way in the current and looks back to see how the others
are faring, without any thought of Bunyan's vision and the
hopes of the dying Christian. Similarly the fisherman
mends his net by the Sea of Galilee without thinking that he

FORDING THE JORDAN.

has a soul to be caught, and the farmer sets up pillars of
rough stone in his vineyard and splashes them with a wash
of lime to gleam in the night and frighten away the jackals,
without thinking that there are far more important grapes to
be protected. And so, busy and expanding Jerusalem of
to-day, with its sects and impostures, has a wall far wider
than the explorer sinks his shaft to discover; its name
Zion now belongs to many nations, and *the city of God*
to the whole world.

(2) *The Oriental mind and landscape.*—The enjoyment
of landscape beauty for its own sake is a modern product
of Western life, and the ordinary Oriental has no eye for
it. His mind is practical rather than æsthetic or scientific.

He accepts devoutly the signs and results of adaptation in the natural world, but he does not trouble about the process. He is indifferent to botany, geology, and archæology, and generally regards the study of secondary causes and the explanation of nature as an impertinence. He is interested in plants for food and medicine, in the forest for fuel, in the hills for health and defence, in ancient ruins for hidden treasure, and in the stars for direction and destiny. Thus Lot was an Oriental artist when he looked upon the plain of Sodom and saw that it was well watered (Gen. xiii. 10); similarly Achsah in her petition for the water-springs of her inheritance (Josh. xv. 19); also Isaac when the woodland smell of Esau's raiment reminded him of "a field which the Lord hath blessed" (Gen. xxvii. 27). Doubtless the ordinary Israelite of ancient times, like the modern Syrian, generally regarded the world around him from the point of view of industrial thrift; it was a world that he had been appointed to till and subdue, and into which labour, as curse or counter-active, had entered because of sin. The modern Syrian simply sees in nature what the heroes of Homer and Virgil usually looked for, namely, fertility and refreshment, the beauty of the abundant crop, and the pleasure of the shading tree and cool fountain. In all likelihood the Israelite of ancient times was the same, with a strong sense of attachment, however, to familiar and favoured localities, as we see in the just pride with which all Israelites regarded Jerusalem, in Naaman's chivalrous protest on behalf of the rivers of Damascus, and in the Samaritan woman's championship of Jacob's well.

(3) *Idolatry and landscape.* — A third reason that affected the outlook upon nature was the surrounding heathen worship of the powers of nature. This polluted the beautiful in creation, just as gambling threatens now to take possession of some of our best in-door games and

out-door recreations. The "high places" of Baal and Ashtóreth had their green trees, cool air, sparkling fountains, and pleasant prospects. In such scenes, away from the common routine, where the sun's heat could not oppress, and the fountain bursting from the cavern spread life and beauty wherever it went, it seemed not only an impulse from within but a call from above to cast aside care, and give the heart up to merriment and revelry. The Israelite had his ancestral seat under the vine-trellis and sweet-scented fig-tree, and his legitimate re-joicings at the Feasts of Pentecost and Tabernacles, but the heart had always a secret and dangerous set towards the festivities of nature-worship. The keeping of the Law, which was their political protection, and the safeguard of the weak against the strong, left a loveless, unfilled place in the common hearts of men. While securing morality, it did not create the joyful, purified heart. Constraint was not comfort, and the law was not life ; and it needed the express prohibitions in the second commandment, and the constant warnings of the prophets, to make Palestine the *Holy* Land, that is, with all its scenery, industries, and institutions *devoted* to the Lord and to Him only. Hence there might have been a note of defiance mingling with the adoration when the Psalmist said, " The heavens declare the glory of *God*" (Ps. xix. 1)—not the grandeur of Baal or the fancies of the heathen soothsayer. Such contamination would tend to alienate the earnest Israelite, and make him suspicious and silent towards the beautiful in nature. This antagonism between holiness and happi-ness was removed when Christ said, " I came that they may have life, and may have it abundantly" (John x. 10), rebuking at once the narrowness of the letter and the heathen debasement of the physical world. Since then the book of the Law has been to us a larger volume than it was to the ancient Israelite ; and nature, delivered from the bondage of idolatry, has given us many beautiful thoughts about the mind of God. At the present day in Syria and Palestine, the Christian monasteries occupy many of the sites of the idolatrous high places, and in cloisters built of the great stones and pillars of the Baal-temples perpetuate the error of the Pharisee—that religion means separation from the world.

The time when Palestine looks greenest and most beautiful is the beginning of April (Song of Solomon ii. 11-13). There is, then, a great simultaneous outburst of flowers—daisies, poppies, and red anemones appearing in astonishing abundance. This sudden and short-lived greenness of the landscape, along with the multitude of bright flowers, is much more impressive in Palestine than in a country where one walks on turf and sees green fields during the greater part of the year. In the month of May it rapidly disappears as the crops ripen and are gathered in, and the plants wither for want of rain. This fact of climate enters into the frequent allusion to the brevity of life in connection with grass and flowers, and it gives a special emphasis to the appeal, "If God so clothe the grass of the field" (Matt. vi. 30). The modern Arabs notice the same features of brevity, profusion, and beauty, saying in their familiar proverbs, "The sons of flesh are like grass," "The troubles of life are more than the grasses of the field," and "Children are the flowers of the world."

7. Weather Changes.—The state of the weather is seldom a topic of conversation among Orientals. The Syrian peasant, when asked as to whether the day is likely to keep fair, usually says, "As the Lord wills," or, with a haphazard look around him, replies, "At present there is no rain." He has not given a thought to the subject, and has no opinion to offer. Among themselves such matters are not referred to in saluting a fellow-traveller on the road. There are several reasons for this reticence : (1) A certain kind of weather is so uniformly characteristic of the different months and periods of the year that the habit of observation is not called for. When there is rain the Oriental says, "This is its time;" when the heat is overpowering he wipes his brow and says, "It is the custom; what can we do?" Hence the wonderfulness of the shower in wheat harvest in the beginning of June, when the rain had ceased, not to return for several months (1 Sam. xii. 17). (2) The introduction of something springing fresh from the actual circumstances of the moment is out of harmony with the dignified but cut-and-dry formalities of Oriental salutation. The weather belongs to nobody, and a reference to it does not lead up to any assurance of good-will, or offer of service, or expectation of benefit. (3) A suspicion of indolence and impiety is apt to attach itself to the critical observation of the signs of the sky. The thought of Eccles. xi. 4 is repeated by the Arabic proverb: "The lazy man becomes an astrologer." A missionary hurrying home in a heavy shower saw from under his umbrella a Moslem friend plodding along unprotected in the wet, and said to him, "This is a dreadful day of rain!" With a solemn upward look the old man replied, "Do you think He does not understand His work?" The wretchedness of the situation could not be disputed, but the thought was that of the patriarch, "Shall we receive good at the hand of God, and shall we not receive evil?" (Job ii. 10).

While the weather does not furnish a topic of conversation in the East, its leading signs are understood and acted upon. In a limited territory like Palestine, bordered by the sea, the desert, and the mountain range, everything with regard to heat and cold, dryness and moisture, depends upon the direction of the wind.

The west wind is the most pleasant and refreshing. It brings clouds and showers from the Mediterranean

(1 Kings xviii. 44 ; Luke xii. 54). At the end of summer there is often a repetition of what happened when Elijah prayed and Gehazi watched on Mount Carmel. A small gray cloud rises over the clear sea-line in the south-west, and the sky becomes rapidly darkened by heavy masses of cloud driven by a strong wind, soon accompanied by thunder and lightning. When this wind begins to blow at this particular time, and the thistledown to fly over the bare fields, the peasants know what to expect, and hurry to the vineyards and housetops to gather in the drying raisins and figs before the rain falls in torrents.

The north wind is remarkable for its power of arresting rain and dispersing clouds. The translation of the Authorised Version in Prov. xxv. 23 has thus the support of the climate. In the Hebrew the word translated "back - biting" means concealment, as the word for " north " means originally the hidden quarter. The sense probably is that as the north wind dispels rain, so a tongue of self-restraint does an angry countenance. This would be true to life and the climate, and in harmony with the context. The north wind deposits its moisture on the Taurus and Lebanon mountains, but brings with it the impurities it has contracted in its passage over towns and malarial districts. It is a cool current of air when it enters Syria, intermittent and gusty in its action. It is local in its area, being chiefly confined to the sea-side plain and nearer slopes ; inland it either dies away in scorching heat or passes into a strong east wind. It is probably owing to these impurities and the unusual combination of cold wind and blazing sunshine that it generally causes headache and neuralgia, and sometimes blights delicate vegetation like a sea-fog. It is called by the Arabs the poison-wind (from *samm*, poison ; hence simoom). Travellers, muleteers, and farmers always rely upon fair weather while it lasts.

The east wind is the usual breeze by night, and as such is cool and dry ; but when it prevails also during the day, or for several days at a time, it becomes exceedingly hot and oppressive, especially when the direction is south-east. It then carries fine sand-dust, giving the sky the appearance of burnished metal, the sky of brass in Deut. xxviii. 23, and sometimes covering it with dull gray clouds (Is. xxv. 5, Jude ver. 12). The heat increases with the elevation, as in the gallery of a crowded theatre or church,—a temperature of 85° in the shade at the sea-side rising to 97° on the Lebanon. On account of its extreme dryness and its being almost as hot during the night as in the day-time, it is very trying to both animal and vegetable life. The thin ears of corn in Pharaoh's dream appeared blasted by it (Gen. xli. 6). The word sirocco (s = sh) preserves the Arabic origin from *shirk*, east, as also appears in the word Saracens—the people of the East. Fortunately this wind seldom lasts long, and its brief visits are usually welcomed in spring, as it causes a rapid advance of vegetation while the ground is still moist, and also in autumn when growth has ceased, and hot weather is needed to dry the fruits for winter preservation before the long summer comes to an end with "the early rain."

The south wind indicates heat (Luke xii. 55), dry if south-east, and soft and relaxing if south-west. It is more uniform in its action, and less characterised by sudden onslaught and hurricane blasts than the north-west and east winds. The west wind is especially dreaded on the Sea of Galilee, often descending suddenly and with the power of a gale, and preventing boats from getting back to the western shore of the lake.

The ordinary action of the wind is to blow from the west in the forenoon, northerly in the afternoon, east in the night, working round by south and returning to the west in the morning, after the sun has been shining for several hours upon the land. This uniformity of the wind was one of the laboured vanities (Eccles. i. 6) of the jaded spirit seeking independent pleasure in creation instead of in the service of God (Eccles. xii. 13). The red sunset (Matt. xvi. 2) indicates the presence of east wind, and is a sign that a season of warm weather may be expected.

The rainfall for the year is about thirty-five inches. The showers are usually much heavier than those in northern countries. In spring and autumn waterspouts are frequently seen over the sea, and sometimes burst on the land, causing much damage to property. As the rain-gauge sometimes records four or five inches to the hour, one can understand what must be the nature of the " overflowing shower " (Ezek. xiii. 11) which causes the walls of gardens to bulge and fall (Ps. lxii. 3), sweeps away stables, affects the foundations of dwelling-houses (Luke vi. 48, 49), and, by the sudden swelling of streams, endangers the lives of men and cattle (Ps. xviii. 16, xc. 5; Is. xxviii. 2, lix. 19). But usually the rain is a shower of blessing and in season (2 Sam. xxiii. 4; Ps. lxxii. 6; Ezek. xxxiv. 36). In the rainless summer the evaporation blown in from the sea during the day settles during the still, cool night in refreshing dew upon the vineyards, fig-trees, olive-trees, and all vegetation, and makes the morning cloud, which lies like a white veil in the valleys for an hour or two after sunrise.

In this land of sunshine so great is the appreciation of moisture in all its forms, that the tenet of ancient philosophy, preserved in the Koran, is still sometimes seen in ornamental relief over city fountains: " *From water We have made all things live.*"

Such are some of the natural conditions by which life in Palestine is affected.

CHAPTER III

The hope of the field is not the heap of the threshing-floor.
Syrian Proverb.

I. PASTORAL LIFE

1. Shepherds and Farmers, their Mutual Relations.— The charge of flocks and the tillage of the soil have always been the two chief employments in Palestine. They were supplementary to each other, one providing clothing, the other food. The Bible makes them equally primitive (Gen. iv. 2). The home life was affected by them; they created the trades, and shaped the civilisation of the villages and towns. In the Bible the duties and dangers of the shepherd, and the methods and implements of the farmer, are constantly referred to when natural objects are used to explain and emphasise spiritual truths.

But while the two flourished side by side, of equal antiquity, and mutually helpful, they were rival competitors for the soil, and wherever an exclusively pastoral class came in contact with an exclusively agricultural class the relationship became one of distrust and defiance. This was chiefly owing to the nature of the land itself and the position of the Israelites in it.

There were plains and valleys for corn, but they lay open on all sides to the sheep and goats. With the exception of vineyards and vegetable gardens, the fields were never protected by walls and fences. Each man's property had its boundary stones or natural land-marks. There was no rotation of crops; hay was unknown, and there were no fields of meadow-grass. There were hills and wildernesses suitable for pasture, but to whom did they belong? If strangers wished to occupy them, who could hinder them? The shepherd's chief thought was to feed his sheep, and he naturally wanted as much of the land as he could get for that purpose. He did not remain in one place, but moved with the season of the year, taking his flock to the higher hills in the hot summer, and in winter going southwards and descending to the warmer plains. Jacob put three days' journey between his own and Laban's flocks, and Jacob's sons setting out from Hebron went as far north as Shechem and Dothan.

The different villages had common access to the uncultivated lands around them, and as their flocks were in the charge of their owners, or of keepers appointed by them, any trespass upon the local corn-fields, or any act of oppression, could be punished by village law. But the case was different when a large pastoral encampment like that of Abraham with over three hundred men approached the borders of agriculture. Such shepherd bands came in force, and as they passed along did not scruple to send their flocks among the standing corn, or to reap and carry off the ripe harvest of the farmer. These were *the Children of the East*, now called the Bedawîn, who are always referred to in the Bible as a menace to social rights and civilised life. Where there was no central government ruling over all each class attended to its own interests, and might was right. It was the penalty that Israel paid for failing to possess the whole land of promise, that it had on its eastern border the lawless pastoral tribes who, whenever the kingdom was brought low by internal strife or war with its neighbours, were always ready to pour in and recover lost ground.

Such was the class difference and rivalry of interest in the soil that separated agriculture and the shepherd life. Owing to the danger from this cause, the citizenship of the village formed not so much a municipality for the management of internal affairs as a sort of militia for resisting outside oppression.

The sheikh of the wandering tribe was met by the sheikh of the village, and in this way the village was able to receive strangers either as guests to be welcomed with honour, or as enemies to be driven off.

To this day when one inquires as to the population of a certain village, the answer is given in military terms that it has so many guns. Its fighting power is its population. On the pastoral side it has been the same ever since Israel marched out of Egypt.

Thus shepherds from a distance, like the patriarchs Abraham, Isaac, and Jacob, with their retinue of servants and large flocks, had to make a covenant with the local authorities. Abraham strengthened his position by alliance with Aner, Eschol, and Mamre. Lot seems to have identified himself with Sodom and its peasant proprietors, leaving his tent, and dwelling in a house within the city gate.

2. The Shepherd's Outfit.—In the Bible the allusions to shepherd life and the figurative terms borrowed from it refer chiefly to its peaceful aspects. Its enemies were wild animals and robbers. The chief occasion of strife among the shepherds, as among the farmers, was connected with the water-supply, the right of access to wells, springs, and brooks (Gen. xiii. 7, xxix. 8; Ex. ii. 17). The care of the flocks and the work of the field flourished side by side. The shepherd belonged to the village, and was maintained in his right to feed his sheep and goats among the rocks and trees of neighbouring hills, and in the corn-fields lying bare after the harvest in May.

The personal appearance of the Eastern shepherd has changed as little as his sheep and his simple duties towards them.

(1) *Cloak.*—He still wraps himself in his large cloak of sheep-skin, or thick material woven of wool, goat-hair, or camel-hair. This protects him from cold and rain by day, and is his blanket at night. The inner pouch in the breast is large enough to hold a new-born lamb or kid

GOURDS AND EARTHEN PITCHERS.

when it has to be helped over rough places, or on account of sickness or injury has to be taken to a place of shelter, or nursed by the family at home (Is. xl. 11).

(2) *Scrip.*—In the summer he may remain in the mountains a month at a time, his only communication with the village being when a fresh supply of bread is brought to him. This he puts into a bag which hangs at his side, the shepherd's scrip (1 Sam. xvii. 40), used also by muleteers and others on a journey. It is a bag made of the dressed skin of a kid, and into it he puts his stock of bread, olives, cheese, raisins, and dried figs.

(3) *Gourd.*—As a drinking-vessel for holding either water or milk he carries a light unbreakable pitcher made of a gourd. Its shape seems to be the original of the vases in glass and earthenware.

(4) *Rod.*—Hanging by his side, or sheathed in a long narrow pouch attached to his cloak, is his oak club. It is carefully chosen, a straight young tree being often torn up for this purpose, and the bulb at the beginning of the root being trimmed to make the head of the club. The handle is dressed to the required thickness, with a hole at the end by which it is tied to the belt, or hangs from the

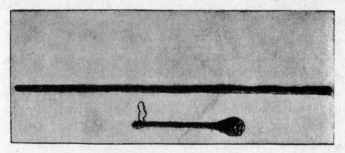

SHEPHERD'S ROD AND STAFF.

wrist like a riding whip. Into the head he drives nails with large heads like those of a horse-shoe. It is the " rod " of Ps. xxiii. 4. It appears in Assyrian sculpture, as the emblem of power in the hand of the king, and was the original of the sceptre, mace, and baton.

(5) *Staff.*—The " staff," mentioned along with the rod in Ps. xxiii., is made of the same wood, but is about 6 feet long, quite plain, rarely with a fork or crook at one end. It is a help in clambering over rocks, in striking off leaves and small branches, in chastising loitering sheep and fighting goats, and on it the shepherd leans as he stands watching his flock. The ordinary walking staff of Orientals is rather longer than that used in the West, is held

by the thin end a few inches from the top, and serves the double purpose of rod and staff, a weapon of defence and a support when standing or walking. Such was the staff in the hand of the prophet as he journeyed from place to place (2 Kings iv. 29)—a peaceful help on the toilsome and dusty road. The two uses, for leaning upon and for striking, are contrasted in Ex. xxi. 19, 20. Both are included in the metaphors suggested by it. Pharaoh is com pared to an untrustworthy staff of bruised reed (Is. xxxvi. 6); and bread is a staff (Ps. cv. 16) "which strengtheneth man's heart" (Ps. civ. 15).

(6) *Sling.*—The shepherd's sling, with which David was familiar, and in the use of which the men of Benjamin were so skilful (Judg. xx. 16), was made of goat-hair. The pad for the stone was of a rounded, diamond shape, with a small slit in the middle, so that when a stone was pressed into it, it closed around like a bag. It received its name in Hebrew, as in Arabic, from the slightly con-cave form in which it was woven. It was "the hollow of a sling" (1 Sam. xxv. 29, R.V.) In the two strings strands of white and black hair were artistically interwoven, one of them at least having an opening at the end for the fingers. Besides being used against robbers and wild animals, it did the work of the Western sheep-dog, for with it the shepherd could drop a stone near a sheep lagging behind, and startle it into a sense of loneliness and danger. At the present day, when a quarrel arises between the youth of neighbouring villages, a sortie of lads is sometimes made from each, and sling-practice is indulged in, usually at long range.

The leading idea of the Oriental sling, in a figurative sense, is distance, rather than accuracy of direction. An Arabic proverb describes the habitual tale-bearer as one who puts a secret in a sling. He tries how far he can throw it. This is the thought of Prov. xxvi. 8, and the translation given in the Authorised Version, and in the margin of the Revised, seems to be the correct one. The more firmly the stone is packed into the sling, the better it is discharged from it, and so it happens when honour is thrust upon a fool, that is, a man who has no idea of religious duty and moral consequences.

The use of the sling was exactly the opposite of that of the scrip—the one throwing out, the other keeping what was put into it. This is probably the meaning of Abigail's words to David, when she contrasted "the bundle of life" and its contents with the sling and its stones (1 Sam. xxv. 29). The man standing in front of her most likely had both his sling and provision-pouch on his person, and while the souls of his enemies would be like stones in the sling, things to be thrown away, his soul would be guarded and kept by the Great Shepherd like the necessaries in the scrip of life. The meaning in one case is so precise and picturesque that an allusion equally exact and obvious is required for the other.

3. **Management of the Flock.**—(1) *The shepherd's presence.*—By day and by night the shepherd is always with his sheep. As already explained, this was necessary on account of the exposed nature of the land, and the presence of danger from wild animals and robbers. One of the most familiar and beautiful sights of the East is that of the shepherd leading his sheep to the pasture. He often has a dog or two with him, especially in the lonely and remote parts of the mountain pasture. But these are large, fierce animals, that can offer battle to the wolf, and by night give warning of the approach of thieves. He depends upon the sheep to follow, and they in turn expect him never to leave them. They run after him if he appears to be escaping from them, and are terrified when he is out of sight, or any stranger appears instead of him. He calls to them from

3

time to time to let them know that he is at hand. The
sheep listen and continue grazing, but if any one else tries
to produce the same peculiar cries and guttural sounds,
they look around with a startled air and begin to scatter.

(2) *The shepherd's protection.*—As he is always with
them, he is constantly providing for them.   He is not
only ready to protect them, but conducts them to the most
suitable ground by the best way ; gives them music on his
reed flute, to which the younger ones sometimes respond
by capering around him ; strips leaves from the branches ;
leads them at noon to the shelter of a cliff, or to the shade
of a walnut or willow tree beside the well or brook ; and
in every possible way lives among them and for them.
At sunset he conducts them back to the fold, where, during
the night, they may lie down in safety, and mix with
several other flocks.

The sheepfold is often a large cave, or an enclosure in
a sheltered hollow made by a rough stone wall, which has,
along the top, a formidable fringe of thorns like furze and
blackthorn, kept in position by stones laid upon it.   At
the mouth of the cave, or at the side of the wall near
the entrance, the shepherds have a covered place made of
branches, a tabernacle such as Peter wished to make on the
Mount of Transfiguration, and here, as on the night of the
Nativity at Bethlehem, they keep watch over their flocks
by night.   The sheep require this constant and complete
protection, as they have no thought of defending themselves.   While goats, on the appearance of a wolf, will
run together and form a solid mass, with horns to the
front, the sheep are immediately scattered and fall an easy
prey (John x. 12).

One of the most interesting sights of shepherd life is
to watch a flock fording a stream.   The shepherd leads as
usual, and the sheep follow in a string at his heels, but in
the middle of the stream they begin to lose their footing

and drift with the current. The shepherd hurries forward, grasping first one and then another, pushing as many as he can reach in front of him and hauling others up against the pressure of the water. As soon as he reaches the opposite side he hastens along the bank and draws out those that have been swept down, and have reached the other side faint with the struggle. The sheep fare best that keep nearest the shepherd. Such a deliverance seems to be referred to in Ps. xviii. 16, " He took me, He drew me out of many waters."

(3) *The shepherd's knowledge.*—As he is always with them, and so deeply interested in them, the shepherd comes to know his sheep very intimately. Many of them have pet names suggested either by the appearance or character of the particular sheep, or by some incident connected with it. At sunset the sheep are counted, usually two by two ; but as a rule when they are brought together, the absence of any one is immediately *felt*. It is not only that one sheep is amissing, but the appearance of the whole flock seems to want something. This knowledge is so intimate and instinctively reliable that the formality of counting is often dispensed with. One day a missionary, meeting a shepherd on one of the wildest parts of the Lebanon, asked him various questions about his sheep, and among others if he counted them every night. On answering that he did not, he was asked how he knew if they were all there or not. His reply was, " Master, if you were to put a cloth over my eyes, and bring me any sheep and only let me put my hands on its face, I could tell in a moment if it was mine or not." Such is the fulness of meaning in the words of the Good Shepherd, " I know mine own, and mine own know Me " (John x. 14).

There is, however, the hireling shepherd, and he is as notorious for unfaithfulness as the true shepherd is for fidelity to his charge. His witness, like that of a pigeon-

breeder (on account of using decoys) is not accepted in an
Oriental law-court.   He is in a position of duty, without
any sense of duty, and no one to watch how he does it.
Prowess can get no praise, and desertion can be screened
by lies.   He receives very little pay, and he has frequent
opportunities of selling kids and sheep to passing travellers,
or of sending them to the market by the hand of relatives.
And at the end of the season he accounts for them as
stolen by Bedawîn, devoured by wolves, or fallen from
precipices.

The shepherd's season of rejoicing is at the time of
sheep-shearing in May and June.   The flocks have been
increased by the season's lambs; milk, butter, and cheese
are abundant; pasture is still plentiful for those who
know where to seek it, and the warm summer weather
makes out-door life delightful by day and night.   It is
the time of invitations and feasting both among the
Bedawîn and the shepherds of the villages.   It was
most probably at such a time that Job's sons met for
festivity.   The same celebration is referred to in Gen.
xxxi. 19, xxxviii. 13, and 1 Sam. xxv. 2.

As might be expected from a calling so important and
familiar to the Israelites, many comparisons and lessons
are drawn from the pastoral life.   The constant presence
of the shepherd among his sheep and his protection of
them were arresting features that were easily transferred
to higher relationships.   Ps. xxiii. remains the simplest
and profoundest expression of trust in God.   The dependence of the sheep upon the shepherd is not a figure
for the beginning of the spiritual life merely—to be left
behind when we know as we have been known; the
redeemed and glorified are still being led to the living
fountains of waters (Rev. vii. 17).

The bond was such that under this form rebellious
Israel could plead, "Why doth thine anger smoke against the

sheep of thy pasture?" (Ps. lxxiv. 1). Everything in the way of devoted love, intimate knowledge, and protective power was summed up in the title, "Jesus that great Shepherd of the sheep" (Heb. xiii. 20). The parables of Luke xv. 3-7 and John x. 1-18 are in the same line. Compare also Ps. lxxix. 13, xcv. 7; Ezek. xxxiv. 8. When Peter was made glad and strong by forgiveness and restoration, the renewed trust of Christ's service was given to him in a form rich with chivalrous associations, "Feed my sheep" (John xxi. 16).

The utter helplessness of sheep without a shepherd is very frequently alluded to in the Bible, and the figure is applied in all its fulness to moral and religious matters, such as the manifold facilities for concealment, loitering and error in the wilderness of life, the losses and sorrows that occur when the will is without definite leading and submission, and the evils that attend both false alarms and real dangers (Num. xxvii. 17; 1 Sam. xxv. 2; 1 Kings xxii. 17; Ps. cxix. 176; Is. liii. 6; Jer. l. 4, 17; Ezek. xxxiv. 6, 12).

Finally, there was the dumb submission of the sheep, when being shorn or about to be killed, that was made the emblem of silent resignation and hopeless doom. Israel could often plead the resemblance of its condition to such sealed fate and calm despair; and the figure enters into the great prophecy of Is. liii. He who sent out His disciples to be "as sheep in the midst of wolves" (Matt. x. 16) was to be first "a Lamb slain" (Rev. v. 12).

II. Agricultural Life

When it is mentioned that French railway trucks are now supplanting the camels in bringing in wheat from the rich plain south of Damascus, that an American engineer is sinking Artesian wells at Sidon for irrigating the land, and that every summer English steamers lie off Gaza loading barley for Scotland, the suspicion naturally arises that the farmer of Palestine has left the shepherd behind, and that his life is no longer a reminder of patriarchal methods. But the land is still a land of corn and wine and oil; and the sowing and reaping, the treading of grapes in the wine-press, the beating of the olive-tree for its berries,—these and many other details of peasant life are the same to-day as when Ruth gleaned and Elisha followed the plough.

1. Grain.—The chief grain-fields are the Syrian plain between Lebanon and Anti-Lebanon, the Hauran east of Galilee, the plains of Esdraelon and Sharon, and the plateau around Jerusalem, Bethlehem, and Hebron. The appearance of the level land without walls, fences, or hedges is that of a great green sea. On the sloping ground, as on the sides of all the watercourse valleys, called wâdies, the land is laid off in stair-like ridges, each leading into the one above or below it so that all can be ploughed continuously. These terraces serve a double purpose; the ground is cleared of rock and large stones in building the low walls, and by the succession of levels the soil is kept in its place and not swept down to the foot of the valley by the winter rains. All over the land there are terraces fallen down, and overgrown, and hardly to be recognised, indicating at once the resemblance and the difference between the ancient and modern civilisations. The cereals sown are chiefly wheat, plain and bearded, barley, and spelt or vetch, translated rye in Ex. ix. 32; Is. xxviii. 25; and in Ezek. iv. 9, fitches. Oats are unknown. Besides the above are millet, beans, and lentils (Ezek. iv. 9), also pulse (Dan. i. 12), under which is included everything of the nature of pease or beans, in fact all seed-food apart from wheat and barley.

(1) *Sowing.*—The time for sowing grain is when the soil has been softened for the plough by the first rains in the beginning of October. Millet, however, is sown in

summer upon irrigated land. When winter comes on
cold and wet, before the barley is put into the ground, it
is sown in the beginning of February. When the soil is
very rough it is customary to plough twice, but ordinarily
the seed is sown and then ploughed in. The farmer
walks in front scattering the seed, and one of the family
or a servant follows immediately with the plough. In
the parable the seed that fell on the footpath could be

ORIENTAL PLOUGH.

picked up by the birds as it was not covered like the rest
(Matt. xiii. 4).

The levelling-up of the ground in terraces often causes
broad slabs of rock to be thinly covered over with soil.
Thorns abound everywhere, growing with great rapidity
and strength. They are either collected and burnt on the
field, or used as fuel, or ground on the threshing-floor as
fodder for the cattle (Matt. xiii. 5-7).

Barley is ripe in April and May, wheat in May and
June, there being much variety as to time, owing to
difference in elevation from the Jordan valley to the fields
around the cedars over 6000 feet above the sea. The
latter rains in March refresh the standing crops, delaying

the time of harvest, but filling out the grain before it
finally ripens.   A field of wheat or barley has the pale
white appearance of oats at home.   The rain has ceased
for three months and the stalks and ears become perfectly
dry.

(2) *Harvest.*—The stalks are either cut with the sickle
or torn up by the roots, and the sheaves are carried to the
threshing-floors on the backs of men, donkeys, horses, and

THRESHING-FLOOR.

camels, carts not being used for this purpose as they once
were (Am. ii. 13).   The chief perils to the crop apart
from the nature of the soil and the hands of robbers, are
from mildew or sweating in soft misty weather, or blasting
by the dry heat of the east wind (Deut. xxviii. 22;
2 Chron. vi. 28; Am. iv. 9), and occasionally from locusts.

Though the crops in Syria do not present such an
appearance of solid mass as in Egypt, the soil is in many
places exceedingly fertile, and the return corresponds with
the standards cited in the parable (Matt. xiii. 8).

(3) *Threshing.*—The threshing-floor is a circular piece of

level ground about 20 to 30 feet in diameter, in an open, breezy locality near the village. The ground is carefully levelled and cleaned, and has around it a roughly-placed row of large stones to keep the straw from being scattered about. Sheaves are unbound and sprinkled over it, till the straw lies about a foot deep. The simplest mode of threshing is to drive cattle and donkeys over the dry straw, but the contrivance of the threshing-board is generally

THRESHING AND WINNOWING INSTRUMENTS.

resorted to. This consists of thick planks nailed together, making an oblong of 5 by 4 feet, having lumps of rough basaltic rock let into the under-surface of the boards. Less frequently it is a wooden frame furnished with small wheels below it. A pair of oxen are yoked to it, and a man stands upon it, goad in hand, and drives the oxen round from morning till evening. These are the oxen that must not be muzzled, but are allowed to pick up straws as often as they wish to do so (Deut. xxv. 4; 1 Cor. ix. 9; 1 Tim. v. 18). When sufficiently threshed the

broken straws, grain, and chaff are piled up in the centre
of the threshing-floor, more sheaves are sprinkled over the
surface, and the threshing is resumed till the work is
done, or there is no room for more in the centre of the
ring.

(4) *Winnowing.*—This is done by the shovel and the fan
(Is. xxx. 24). The fan is a simple wooden pitchfork. By
it the compound of straw, chaff, and grain is tossed in the
air. The chaff flies away over the hillside (Ps. i. 4), and
where it accumulates at the great public threshing-floors it
is burnt up. The straw is deposited a few yards off, while
the grain falls at the feet of the winnower. In this pile
there is still a good deal of husk and straw, and it is at
this concluding stage of the winnowing that the shovel is
brought into use. This work at the threshing-floors is
carried on all day, and from harvest time till the ripened
grapes claim attention in the month of August; and in the
great grain-growing districts it is continued till the close of
September. The owners sleep by the threshing-floors or
appoint watchmen. When the grain is piled into a cone
it is sealed by having a large wooden seal pressed upon it
here and there all around. The attempt to abstract anything would instantly obscure the marks of the seal. The
sealing is either in the interests of the working-partners or
owners, or that the gross yield may remain intact until the
Government official takes his tithe. It is sealed unto the
appointed day of weighing and measuring. The use of
the seal is often referred to in connection with documents
and treasures, as well as with the threshing-floors, and
suggests profound spiritual meanings (Dan. xii. 8; Rom.
xv. 28; Eph. i. 13, iv. 30). Among the peasantry of the
present day any recommendation of a winnowing-machine
is met by the remonstrance that their fathers did it in this
way, and at the winnowing season there is nothing else to
do. The further and final cleansing that the grain under-

goes by means of the sieve we shall speak of in connection
with food and domestic life.

2. The Vineyard.—The vine has always had an important place among the industries of Palestine. Its
culture is one of the leading characteristics of the land
(Deut. viii. 8; Ps. lxxx.; Is. v.; Ezek. xvii.)

(1) *Locality.*—Vineyards are found all over the country,
but the position most suitable is the hillside, or the
gently-sloping ground at the foot of a hill. The vine
likes open, loose soil into which it can sink its deep roots
and reach the moisture that drips down over the surface
of the mountain rock. Above ground it must have plenty
of air and sunshine, and by night the dew rests upon its
leaves refreshingly, but its source of nourishment and
strength is in the deep crevices of the rock beyond the
reach of the sun's heat.

(2) *Preparation.*—The vineyard requires a great deal
of preparatory work. A wall has to be built round it.
The irregular rocky ground has to be laid off in terraces,
one below the other on the slope, varying in width from
1 to 4 or 5 yards; large rocks have to be broken up
and built with other stones into these successive rough
walls, varying in height from 2 to 6 feet. Then, much
more thoroughly than is thought of for the grain fields,
the ground must be cleared of thorns and thistles. In
the case of a large vineyard a winepress has then to be
dug, and a room made for the watchman. The ground
has to be well gone over with the hoe, and repairs on
the terraces have to be attended to. On account of the
constant attention required by the vineyards we read that
at the time of the captivity of Judah, some of the poorest
of the land were left to sow the fields and to keep the
vineyards in order (2 Kings xxv. 12).

The neglected vineyard is described as covered with
thorns and strong hardy weeds, and as having the wall

broken down by the rain torrent (Prov. xxiv. 30, 31). It is the sum total of such labours that is spread to view when the question is asked, "What could have been done more to my vineyard that I have not done in it?" (Is. v. 4.)

(3) *Growth of the vine.*—This is very rapid and luxuriant. The slips are set in the ground about 12 feet or more apart to give space for the running branches. The young vine is cut back and not allowed to bear fruit till after the third year. In April and May the vine blossom is out and gives forth a sweet, delicate perfume (Song of Sol. ii. 13). The branches covered with large richly-green leaves rapidly cover the ground; the tendrils droop over the terrace-walls, run over rocky boulders, or, taking possession of an oak-tree, brighten its quiet foliage with their sparkle and transparency, and wave from its topmost branches in a perfect riot of life and endless energy. It must be a very rich, happy, and triumphant life that is described by the figure, "I am the vine, ye are the branches" (John xv. 5).

(4) *Fruit.*—There may be many kinds of grapes, even in one vineyard, both of the purple and the green sorts. Some villages are celebrated for this variety, one having as many as twelve or twenty different kinds in its vine-yards; others are famous for the perfection to which they have brought one particular kind. There are many forms and varieties of flavour. Names are suggested by something in the size or colouring of the grape or the general appearance of the cluster. Thus we have on Lebanon, *Bride's fingers* (of long tapering form, very smooth and translucent), *Maiden's cheeks* (with a blush of colour on each side), *Mule's head* (a large clumsy-looking purple grape), and *Hen-and-Chickens* (a cluster having large green grapes surrounded by many small seedless ones about the size of currants).

(5) *Uses of the grape.*—(*a*) Fresh ripe grapes, eaten
with bread, form a chief article of food during September
and October. (*b*) Raisins. These are dried in a prepared
levelled corner of the vineyard. During the process of
drying under the sun, they are frequently turned over and
sprinkled with olive oil to keep the skin moist. They are
preserved in bunches or scattered over the ground. They
form an important item of the winter's stores among the

WINEPRESS.

peasantry, and they seem to have been highly valued in
Bible times as a convenient and refreshing article of food
(1 Sam. xxv. 18, xxx. 12; 2 Sam. xvi. 1; 1 Chron. xii.
40). (*c*) Wine and syrup. These were made at the wine-
press, when the grapes were fully ripe and the vintage
season began to near its end in the beginning of October.

The winepress consists of two troughs cut in the solid
rock, with a partition about 3 inches thick left between
them. One is higher than the other, and this upper one
is a large flat square, about a foot or a foot and a half deep.

Here the grapes are thrown in and trodden by the feet of men, women, and children—usually of the same family, or relatives having a joint interest in the vineyard. As they tread they keep time with hand-clapping and snatches of song (Is. xvi. 10 ; Jer. xlviii. 33). Such social gladness contrasts with the case of solitude and sorrow referred to in Is. lxiii. 3. After being thus pressed by the feet, the grape skins are collected into a heap, a large flat stone is laid upon them, and they are subjected to pressure from a large weighted beam. The juice flows into the lower trough through the opening in the partition. It is smaller but deeper ; if the upper be 6 feet long by 5 feet broad, the lower one will be about 4 feet long by 2 feet broad, but about 3 feet deep. If the position of the rock allows it, a hole near the bottom lets off the juice into vessels for collecting it. Some of it is allowed to become sour for use as vinegar. The juice of the dark grape is generally made into claret of a somewhat sour, astringent taste, and that of the white or green grape is boiled a little and made into sweet wine. Some of it is distilled and made into a spirit, which the modern Jews call by a Hebrew name, *burning wine.*

The people of the land know nothing of unfermented wine. There is no custom of drinking newly-strained grape-juice such as might be suggested by the dream of Pharaoh's butler. The meaning evidently is that, dream-like, the wine-making process was in the vision as rapid as the ripening of the grapes. Intemperance is too far-reaching and deep-seated an evil to be settled by the etymology of a word or the customs of one people or country. Orientals are not inclined to intemperance. The warm climate very quickly makes it a cause of discomfort and disease, and under the influence of wine the excitable Orientals are easily tempted into quarrelling and crime. It is regarded as a shameful vice, is of rare

occurrence, and when it does occur is kept out of sight
(1 Thess. v. 7). Wine is entirely forbidden to the
Moslems on account of the moral evil so often connected
with it. In the recitation of poetry and the stories of
the heroes of Islam the bringing in of wine is constantly
referred to, but it is regarded merely as a stage expression
that has nothing to do with real life. The Arabs in their
proverbs speak of it as expelling reason and putting in
its place remorse. When used by Orientals it is in the
winter season and at meals, but while its strengthening
value at certain times is recognised, the habit of wine-
drinking is generally associated with excessive festivity
and abuse.

In the Jewish Prayer-book one of the thanksgivings is
for the creation of the vine, and on the return from the
synagogue, to which in the morning they go fasting, a
glass of wine is drunk with this blessing pronounced over
it. This custom was perhaps alluded to by Peter on the
day of Pentecost as showing the impossibility of intoxication
at 9 A.M.—an hour when Jews had but newly returned
from morning prayer.

Syrup is made by boiling the juice of the grape until
it reaches the consistency of honey. It is intensely sweet,
and, having much the same colour and consistency, it is
in Hebrew called by the same name as honey.

(6) *Dangers to the vineyard.*—The chief enemies are
the locust; the east wind withering the grapes with dry
heat, and the south-west wind bringing up soft mist and
moist warmth from the sea; the wild animals, such as
jackals, foxes, and bears; and the attempts of robbers and
petty thefts of passing travellers. Against men and animals
the watchman is appointed over a vineyard or group of
vineyards. He is there day and night to frighten away
animals and challenge and report upon intruders. He
roams about at night, and in the daytime he has in a

conspicuous spot a booth (Is. i. 8, R.V.) made of four stout poles fixed into the ground, with a boarding lashed across half-way up, and all covered with oak leaves. Here the watchman sits and watches by day. When the season is over and the vineyard bare, the booth gets stripped and bent by the wind and rain, and is a picture of neglect and desolation.

VINEYARD BOOTH.

Such was the daughter of Zion in the time of Isaiah (Is. i. 8). Sometimes a permanent stone-built room takes the place of the booth. It serves both as a watch-tower and a place of shelter, in which the wine can be boiled and syrup made if the weather should prove cold and rainy at the time. Such was the tower of the parable (Matt. xxi. 33).

Pruning has to be done in December or January, not when the vine is in blossom and foliage, as it bleeds so profusely.

Vineyards are either tended by their owners, or are

let out to husbandmen who receive for their labour half of
the produce.

The promise of fruitful seasons (Lev. xxvi. 5) made
the time of corn-threshing in July and August run into
the grape harvest of September and October, and this
again trenched upon the time of ploughing and sowing in
November.

3. The Olive-Tree.—The olive-tree is a very characteristic feature of Oriental landscape. It is of a dusty
silvery gray, and contrasts with the bright pure green
of the mulberry, apricot, orange, and other trees. It
presents many changes of colour as it is seen with the
light upon or against it, in the morning, at mid-day, or at
evening. A grove of olive-trees resembles a clump of
willows or silver birches in foliage, though inferior in the
grace of form and movement of the branches. The dark
stems shine through the branches, and the light red soil
which it likes best gives the warmth of tone which the
tree itself lacks. Such is the beauty of the olive. It
bears fruit after seven years, and is at full fruit-bearing
strength in its fourteenth year. It is fruitful in alternate
years, and one tree will yield from a dozen to twenty
gallons of oil.

The berries are gathered in October, about the time
of the Jewish Feast of Tabernacles. As the trees have
seldom any enclosing wall around them, or those in one
enclosure may have different owners, the sheikh appoints
a day for the gathering, so that each may attend to his
own.

The tree is about twenty feet high and is easily climbed,
and the branches are beaten from the ground by a long
stripped palm branch (Is. xvii. 6, xxiv. 13). Whatever
remains after the appointed day may be gleaned by any
one (Deut. xxiv. 20; Is. xvii. 6).

Old trees have suckers rising from the stem, close to

4

the ground, six or seven, or a dozen or more of them
rising in a circle around the gnarled and often rent bole.
These are the "olive-branches" springing up to take the
place of the parent tree (Ps. cxxviii. 3).

A graft is inserted into the stem of a wild olive, which
for the purpose is cut down near to the ground, and all
below is reckoned as root and feeder.   Hence the grafting
of the heathen Gentile upon the stock of the Bible-
taught Israelite was contrary to nature or custom (Rom.
xi. 24).   Even the planted slip of a fruitful olive is
improved by being cut down and grafted.   It is remarkable for the multitude of blossoms that it casts off (Job
xv. 33).   Olives form the principal accompaniment and
relish of the bread of the labouring man.   Bread and
olives in Syria correspond to the porridge and milk of
Scotland.   Hiram's workmen were supplied with them
(2 Chron. ii. 10).   Olive oil is extensively used in soap-
making and cooking.   The wood was used in Solomon's
temple (1 Kings vi. 31), and is still in Jerusalem put to
ornamental uses.

4. Fig-Trees.—These take rank after the vines and
olive-trees in number and fruit-bearing value, although
at the present day the most important after wheat and
barley is the mulberry-tree, as its leaves are the food of
the silkworm.

(1) *Appearance.* — The olive, fig, and pomegranate
trees, and also the larger walnut and locust-bean trees,
while differing in the colour of their foliage, are all wide-
spreading, well-filled trees, and at a distance resemble
large apple and pear trees, the pomegranate being usually
rather smaller and more like an elder-tree in form and
size.   When stripped of its leaves the fig-tree looks like
a mere tangle of ropes, but by this multitude of small
branches a great many points are presented to the sunlight, and in summer these are all studded with figs and

screened over with large leaves. The tree affords a pleasant shelter beside the house, and in this connection is mentioned in the Bible along with the trained vine (1 Kings iv. 25; Mic. iv. 4; John i. 48).

(2) *Fruit.*—There may be said to be three fig seasons. (a) Early figs. These are few in number, and it is not every tree that has them. They are ripe a month before the regular crop. They are not really better than the ordinary summer figs, being indeed rather inferior in flavour though large and juicy, but they are esteemed a delicacy because they are the first of the season and limited in quantity. They are often sent by the owner of the tree as a present to his friends. This appreciation and the fact that they fall off easily, are noticed in the Bible, and are made to point to moral resemblances (Hos. ix. 10; Jer. xxiv. 2; Nah. iii. 12). (b) Ordinary summer figs. These are extensively used for food in August and September, and when dried on the flat house-tops are stored for winter use (1 Sam. xxv. 18, xxx. 12). (c) Winter figs. These mature slowly, and remain along with the deep-green leaves on the tree until late in autumn, or even to the end of the year. They are large and fleshy, but inferior in flavour to those of the summer season. The quantity of them is comparatively small, though much larger, of course, than that of the early figs.

While good figs are very good, bad figs can be very bad. They may become dry and shrivelled, gluey and insipid, or infected by small worms (Jer. xxiv. 8).

(3) *The fig-tree as a sign of the season.*—The fig-tree comes into foliage later than the almond, apricot, and peach trees, and when its tender leaves are unsheathed, and expand and deepen in colour, it is a sign that summer days are at hand (Matt. xxiv. 32; Mark xiii. 28). At the time of opening buds and blossoms the fig-tree sends out a peculiar odour, like sweetly-perfumed incense. It is

this fragrance, like that of the sweet spices used in embalming, that seems to be indicated among the signs of approaching summer in Song of Solomon ii. 13. There the literal meaning of the word translated "putteth forth," and "ripeneth," R.V., is that of perfuming and giving scent.

(4) *The fig-tree that withered* (Matt. xxi. 19; Mark xi. 13).—We have all at times felt secret drawings of sympathy towards this tree as we have also at times towards Esau, Saul, Joab, and a few others. Now, in order to understand the case of the fig-tree, the first thing to attend to is the fig-tree's law of growth and fruit-bearing. What is it? It is that leaves and fruit appear together and disappear together. As soon as the leaves begin to bud the figs begin to form.

At the end of summer some of the figs may survive the leaves around them at the tips of the branches, but the presence of leaves is uniformly a guarantee of fruit. It is instructive to compare this tree and its fate with the other fig-tree mentioned in the parable (Luke xiii. 6-9). It also was unfruitful, and had been so for three years, but it was a case of simple failure under ordinary circumstances, at the ordinary season. It is made to teach a different lesson—a lesson of forbearance and encouraging trust.

But with regard to the tree on the Mount of Olives, we are told that it was not yet the time of figs (Mark xi. 13). This fact, which seems at first to excuse the tree, was what really led to its condemnation. If it was not the time of figs, it was not the time of foliage. The tree was in advance of its companions as to leaves, and by its own law of life, that is, the custom of having foliage and figs at the same time, such leadership in outward show should have been accompanied by a similar forwardness in fruit-bearing. But "He found nothing thereon, but leaves only." It was a vegetable Sanhedrim. It seemed to be possessed by the spirit that created the long robe and large phylactery-box. Sins against God were bad enough, but Pharisaism claimed to be for God. Pharisee and fig-tree were alike as to profession without practice. It was the only thing that called forth the stern indignation of Christ.

"Scribes, Pharisees"—and this unnatural fig-tree— "hypocrites!"

Our Lord said, "I am the Truth" (John xiv. 6), and to love Him is to become like Him. Among the things that we are exhorted to think upon, the first place is given to "Whatsoever things are true" (Phil. iv. 8).

5. **Gardens.**—The usual Oriental garden is a walled enclosure for fruit-trees as the vineyard is for vines. There is no thought of flowers, bordered walks, or green turf. The ground is made level, or arranged in a series of levels by low terrace walls, it is then laid out in narrow, shallow drills and irrigated. As each furrow gets its sufficiency of water it is closed at the end by the hoe and naked foot. This may be the reference to watering by the foot in Deut. xi. 10; or the contrast between Palestine and Egypt there indicated may point to some kind of tread-mill wheel for lifting water from the river or canal that it might be distributed over the land. Near towns, and where the water-supply is abundant, there are gardens for vegetables which are cultivated in great abundance and variety.

The usual garden trees are olive, fig, orange, lemon, citron, pomegranate, palm, almond, apricot, peach, banana, and occasionally apple and pear trees. Olive and fig trees are planted sufficiently apart to allow of wheat or barley being sown between them. Olive-trees are thus seen in the garden at the foot of "the green hill," where a rock-cut tomb is situated that is thought by many to have been the tomb of Christ (John xix. 41).

The almond-tree bursts into blossom in the short, dark, cold days of January and amid the blustering winds at the beginning of February. As its flowers are out before the leaves appear, its snowy array seems to emphasise the leafless desolation of the world around it (Eccl. xii. 5).

The apple of Scripture is sometimes thought to be rather the citron or quince ; the term may be a somewhat general one, but the translation given in the Bible has in its favour the fact that the same word in Arabic means an apple. The palm-tree towers aloft among the foliage of the sea-side plain, and rises picturesquely among the villages in the lower valleys. In Arabic poetry and compliment it is the standard simile with regard to stateliness and elegance (Ps. xcii. 2 ; Song of Sol. vii. 7 ; Jer. x. 5).

The walnut and locust-bean trees are often found outside of garden enclosures, either belonging to the owner of the ground or the common property of the village. Locust-beans are ground like olives and the boiled syrup is mixed with figs for winter use. The walnut or nut-tree is found in many localities, but prefers a mountain-valley with its roots beside the brook or spring (Ps. i. 3). It affords a dense and delightful shade, the leaves being refreshingly aromatic (Song of Sol. vi. 11).

Sycamore-trees are often met with singly by the roadside, of gigantic size, and with wide-spreading arms.

Their figs are insipid in taste, about the size of a gooseberry, and growing thick upon small leafless twigs springing out from the trunk and principal branches. They are eaten only by the poorest of the people (Amos vii. 14).

6. Gleaning.—The ancient rules about gleaning are not now observed so carefully as they used to be. On the small farms the harvest field is gleaned very thoroughly by the owners, but a small corner is sometimes left unreaped out of religious scruple. Recently a Scotch engineer took an American reaping-machine to the great wheat plain between the Lebanon ranges, to exhibit its powers to the assembled sheikhs and landowners. He astonished and delighted them, but was mobbed by the poor labourers and gleaning women, who saw that such clean quick work left nothing for them.

In a grove of olive-trees belonging to several owners, and where no walls ever separate one person's property from that of another, gleaning is allowed after the day or days publicly announced for the beating of the trees (Deut. xxiv. 20) and the gathering of the fruit. A similar permission generally holds good among the vines and fig-trees after the Feast of the Cross, which occurs towards the end of September.

From the above it will be seen that with regard to pastoral and agricultural life in Bible times the people now living in Syria and Palestine need no commentary on such matters. Their traditional customs and surrounding conditions not only explain and confirm such references, but help to make the spiritual teaching in connection with them more interesting and impressive.

CHAPTER IV

TRADES AND PROFESSIONS

The hand of **Honour** is a balance,
All roads lead to the flour mill.—*Syrian Proverbs.*

ONE of the happiest sights in family life is to watch the
bright, instantaneous way in which a child awakes out of
sleep, rejoicing that the darkness is past and a new day
has come.   City life in the East shows this feature of
childhood.   The stars of the dawn melt away rapidly in
the increasing light, and as soon as the sun arises the
day's work begins.   The first to be astir are the bakers,
firing the cakes that are sold in the streets, with hot milk,
to the early labourers.   Those who have charge of horses,
mules, donkeys, and camels stretch themselves and rise,
ready-dressed, to prepare the food for which their animals
have been waiting patiently.   Day-labourers, with or
without tools, begin to assemble in the accustomed place,
salute each other, and stand waiting to be engaged.
Workers from the suburbs of the town pour in on foot
and on donkey-back.   The sound of the anvil is heard,
the clinking of the coppersmith at his work, the whirr of
the wheel in the open yard where string is twisted, then
the loud fumbling in the lock as the door of the Arab
shop is opened, and so the new, noisy, bright, busy day
begins.   As soon as the sun sets the work ceases, the
shops are closed, the streets grow empty, and the town

settles down to the rest and silence of another night (Ps. civ. 23).

The Bedawi shepherd is lost in wonder when he enters the town and sees life under conditions so different from his own. His own wants are so few and simple, and the necessaries of food, clothing, and tools are mostly supplied by his own hands and the labours of his family. But in the town each craft has its own street or market-place; the coppersmiths and silversmiths, the sellers of grain, wood, vegetables, mutton, and cloth, makers of shoes and mattresses, are all grouped together, each industry in its own place. It is the distribution of energy and development of special skill that must always come with expanded life.

The trades of the East are remarkable for the skill shown in the use of simple tools, the excellent work produced by rude appliances. The history of Oriental handicrafts is one of expert masters rather than of improved methods. This delicacy of touch, facility in designing, and good eye for proportion and effect, are largely due to the ancient trade-guilds, in which the same work was usually engaged in by father and son from generation to generation. With regard to any improvement in the processes of the work, a trade secret was also a family secret, and was closely guarded. The private profit which thus secured efficiency had its element of danger to the public, as we see to-day in the lost arts of the ancient lacquer-work and the tempering of bronze.

Recent contact with European machinery and manufacture has added a few new occupations, and to some extent modified the old. In Syria and Palestine as elsewhere art exists not for art merely, but for the profit that can be made out of it. This is the moral responsibility of inventions. Orientals are now as fond of our flashy and fading aniline dyes as we are of their rich and

permanent tones in cloth and carpets. The one great
trade that is now awanting is that of the image-maker.
Perhaps the last trace of it is seen in the silver lamps and
vessels that are made as votive offerings for the churches
and saint-shrines, and the six-foot candles of the altar that
supplement the Syrian sunshine.

Let us now turn our attention to some of these trades
and industries, and as we do so we shall be surprised to
find in how many places the Bible will be opened, and
how interesting and helpful these allusions will be
to us.

1. Weaving, Dyeing, and Embroidery.—(1) *Weaving*
is still found in its simplest form among those who were
the first to begin it, namely, the wandering shepherds or
Bedawîn. A Bedawi woman stuffs a bunch of *goat-hair*
under her arm, and drawing out a tuft of it ties it to a
stone. She spins it round and gradually adds more hair.
She thus gets a roughly uniform thread, the twisted strand
that is woven into hair-cloth for the nose-bags of donkeys,
horses, and camels, sacks for holding grain and flour ; and
the lengths that are over-edged and joined together to
make the black "houses of hair"—the Bedăwi tents.
This is the sackcloth of the Bible, which was worn as a
mark of penitence or grief, and was the standard simile for
anything intensely black. Somewhat softer and more
flexible is the cloth of *camel-hair ;* the softest and most
valuable being that of *sheep's wool.* As sheep and goats
are black or white, and camels buff-coloured or dark brown,
decoration is introduced in the form of broad alternate
stripes of light and dark colour. Through all Oriental
weaving we find these two features, the suspended stone-
weight and the love of striped ornamentation. Among
the pastoral tribes the weaving of tent-cloth, the outer
large cloak, and a few similar things, is still the work of
the women. Among the village peasantry also a woman

is often seen twisting thread of cotton or wool as she walks along, but the supply of cloth is now chiefly from the looms of such towns as Aleppo, Beyrout, and Damascus, or imported from Europe. In the Oriental hand-loom, the foundation threads of the warp are fixed to a beam near the root of the room, and slope downwards and forwards in close parallel lines to a horizontal revolving beam at the feet of the weaver. These give the length and breadth of the cloth, and the woof threads of cotton, linen, silk, or wool are one by one passed through them from side to side, each line being pressed into position by a wooden bar brought down upon the web. The weaver sits at his work.

(2) *Dyeing.*—Many of the Oriental dyes are extremely rich and permanent. The brilliant crimson, their favourite colour, is named in Arabic as in Hebrew from the insect that makes the nut in a kind of oak-tree. Indigo is prepared from the rind of the pomegranate. The shell-fish, from which the precious Phœnician "purple" was made that Lydia sold (Acts xvi. 14), is still met with on the beach at Acre.

Bright crimson and soft, faded-looking blue, "dragon's-blood" (Turkey) red, canary yellow, and indigo, with here and there a softening of the sacred Moslem green, the whole broken up and relieved with white—such, ever moving and yet remaining always the same, is the motley effect of an Oriental crowd.

Orientals are very sensitive to light and dark, warm and cold values in colour, but do not feel quite as we do about the relationship of primary and secondary colours of the same strength. Scarlet and purple, blue and green are constantly placed side by side (Ex. xxvi. 1). If a Moslem woman, dressed for the festival, were to appear among the ladies of an English or American drawing-room, they would regard her as decidedly spectacular, while she would wonder what evil some of them had done or suffered that they should dress so soberly. In her own land her dress is a response to the bright sunshine which harmonises everything. Even the zebra in its own haunts is made invisible by its stripes. Along with such bright and often glaring colours, Oriental fabrics have many

CHEQUER-WORK.

subtle shades of gray and olive, delicate flushes of lilac and opal, and salmon-pink like the heart of almond-blossom.

(3) *Embroidery, broidered work.*—This is the orna-mentation of any kind of cloth, cotton, linen, silk, or wool

by different colours and designs. There are two principal kinds.

(*A*) *Monochrome design,* or the effect of a pattern without any additional colour. Here also there are two varieties. (*a*) *On the cloth.*—This is a very intricate and tedious kind of needlework, seldom attempted except **for**

BROIDERED-WORK.

the robe or dress-coat of Oriental male costume. The robe of dressing-gown shape, made of smooth bright linen or coloured silk, is cut out and laid upon its lining of white cotton. Then threads of cotton-twist, like merchant's cord, are laid between and sewn in according to pattern in zig-zags, squares, curves, etc. The sewing running close along each side of the string gives a raised effect like fine

quilting in the yoke of a lady's dress, or as is seen on a
larger scale in our manufactured white bed-covers of the
honeycomb pattern, except that the Oriental cloth is
exactly the same on both sides. Such work upon linen or
silk under bright sunlight is very rich and lustrous; when
upon cloth of gold (Ps. xlv. 13) the effect would be exceedingly resplendent. (*b*) *In the cloth.*—Here the same
style of pattern in lines, squares, circles, zig-zag, and
key-pattern is obtained in the process of weaving without
any raising of the surface. It is woven in Damascus in
a great variety of beautiful designs, and is the familiar
damask of home manufacture. Something of this kind
(*a*) or (*b*) must have been the material and style of the
high priest's coat (Ex. xxviii. 39). It is "*chequer work.*"

(*B*) *Design in different colours* — (*a*) *With raised
surface.*—This was a superadded pattern in gold thread
and different colours. The appearance is that of embossing in metal, as when an Oriental bridal dress of rich,
heavy silk is ornamented with large gold lilies in massive
relief. (*b*) *In the cloth.*—The coloured design is in this
case introduced during the weaving, the prevailing form
of decoration, as in the tabernacle curtains, being that of
stripes.

These Eastern fabrics are usually the same on both
sides. They are called in the Bible "broidered-work
of divers colours" when the chief impression is that of
rich and varied colouring. It is the work of the
variegator (Ex. xxvi. 36; Ezek. xvi. 10). The further
descriptive term "cunning-work" is added when a chief
feature of the elaboration consists in the beauty and
intricacy of the design, the interweaving of geometrical
figures, effects of chain armour and tartan crossings, and
drawings of human, animal, or floral design in the
pattern. It is the work of the designer (Ex. xxvi. 1,
xxviii. 6, xxxvi. 8).

2. Masonry.—Many of the most wonderful antiquities of the East, like its most characteristic present-day features, are due to the work of the mason. His implements and methods are further interesting to the student of Scripture because of its frequent reference to them by way of illustration and teaching.

The farmers everywhere are skilful in the building of the low terrace walls of undressed stone for their corn-fields and vineyards, but when a building has to be constructed of stone and lime the experience of the master mason is usually resorted to. Certain villages are famous for their masons, who travel all over the land fulfilling their engagements.

(1) *The foundation.*—Great attention has to be paid to this on account of the shrinkage and expansion of the ground by summer drought and winter rain. The necessity of getting down to the rock often involves a great deal of labour and expense, and is the most frequent cause of the disappointment referred to in Luke xiv. 9. Deep broad trenches are cut and filled with thick walls of stone and lime. These are carried up to the surface of the ground and allowed for a time to dry and settle. All this work is of course afterwards invisible ; hence the implied discourtesy of building upon another man's foundation (Rom. xv. 20 ; 1 Cor. iii. 10).

(2) *The corner-stone.*—When the first tier of oblong stones is laid upon the foundation prepared for it, a broad square one is chosen for each corner so as to make a sure foundation where the two walls meet (Is. xxviii. 16 ; Ps. cxviii. 22 ; Matt. xxi. 42). A similar square block, but thinner, is often placed at each corner of the top row of stones on which the roof beams are to be laid. Its un-inviting shape would naturally cause this stone to be passed by when the masons were trimming the ordinary oblong stones, until a special need revealed its special fitness

for clasping the two walls. When laying the foundation of an important building for a government office or public institution, the Moslems are accustomed to kill one or more sheep as a feast to the poor. It is the dedication ceremony.

(3) *The measuring reed.*—At the laying of the foundation row, and from time to time during the construction of the walls, the master mason uses a long straight cane, about 20 feet in length, for measuring the spaces of the walls

MASON'S TOOLS.

and between the windows and doors (Ezek. xl. 3 ; Rev. xxi. 16). A somewhat shorter reed or cane is used very simply, but with wonderful correctness, in the building of the arches that are so numerous in Oriental architecture.

(4) *The plumb-line.*—This is a small inverted cone of lead attached by a cord to a cylindrical piece of wood of the same diameter, so that when the wood is laid to the stone newly set in the row the lead suspended below should barely touch the wall. It is in constant use for preserv-

ing the perpendicular. To stand this test is the secret of permanence. Whatever is "off the straight" must fall to the ground however many sheep may have been sacrificed at its dedication (Is. xxviii. 17 ; Jer. xxii. 13). In its moral application this teaching of uprightness applies very specially to "God's building" (1 Cor. iii. 9), the building founded upon holy faith (Jude 20), and the erection of the "spiritual house" (1 Peter ii. 5).

(5) *The levelling-line.*—This is used along with the plumb-line. When a fresh course is to be laid on, two stones of the same height are placed at each end of the wall, or about 20 feet apart, and each is tested for the perpendicular by the plumb-line. Then a length of cord is unwound from its pin and passed several times round one of the stones, and stretched from its outside top corner to the same point of the other stone where it is also made fast. About the middle point of this string the plumb-line is applied again, and then the whole course is laid on, thus securing both perpendicular and horizontal accuracy. This levelling-line seems to be referred to in 2 Kings xxi. 13, where it is prophesied that the line that had been passed over Samaria and the house of Ahab would be stretched over Jerusalem, that is, it would be made level with the ground.

These details of the measured foundation, and the use of the line, and the festivities of the dedication, are alluded to in Job xxxviii. 4-7.

(6) *Tools of the mason.*—These are seen in the accompanying illustration, and are variously adapted to splitting, chipping, and facing the stones. The hammer with the toothed edge is especially interesting, from the fact that the gigantic stones of Baalbek show a graining that must have been produced by a similar instrument.

The small basket for carrying off earth is also of interest, inasmuch as it is found with its hoisting ropes preserved underground through the centuries, and lying where it had been laid down by the toilers of ancient Egypt.

3. Carpentry.—Oriental custom does not make such an extensive demand upon the carpenter as it does upon the mason. His chief work is in making roofs, doors, window-shutters, lattice-squares, and divan frames for the houses. Along the coast there is a small industry in boat building.

Chairs and tables are referred to in the Bible, and their construction is described on the Egyptian monuments, but it is likely that the ordinary peasants, in ancient times as at present, sat and ate on the floor or the divan. In carrying loads the pack-saddle takes the place of the waggon, and gardens are marked off by boundary-stones, walls, and hedges of wild cactus or reed, so that here also the work of the carpenter is not required. The scarcity of timber in certain localities, such as Jerusalem, causes many houses to be covered with a vault or dome of stone instead of a wooden roof.

The ancient Egyptian monuments show the adze, saw, square, awl, and glue-pot, as the chief necessaries of the ancient carpenter, and with these and a few additional implements, his modern successor in the East does his simple work. His most ornamental work is in the panelling of the roof, the making of lattice for the windows, and the arabesque decoration of doors. The adze is his favourite implement. In ripping a board with the saw, he sits on the board and saws away from himself.

An avaricious man is compared by the Arabs to the long double-handed saw for cutting logs into boards, because it "eats" both in going up and coming down.

4. Metal-work.—All the records of the East abundantly support the Bible in indicating that from the earliest times there has been a knowledge of plain and ornamental work in the various metals connected with mechanical art. The ornamental work is called engraving, and corresponds in wood, stone, metal, and jewels to the effect of embroidery in cloth (Ex. xxviii. 11;

ENGRAVING IN WOOD AND METAL.

1 Sam. xiii. 19; 2 Sam. v. 11). It exists at the present day in all the forms referred to in the Bible, in the etched line of the graving tool (Ex. xxxii. 4), in punched-out design, embossing, perforation, the combined effect of

removal and insertion in inlaying and mosaic work, and the complete removal of the carved object, as in the ancient image (Ex. xxxii. 4, xxxix. 14; 1 Kings vi. 18; Ezek. viii. 10; Acts xvii. 29).

The East has always been famous for colossal masonry, but recent exploration in Egypt has revealed that there was equal skill in the most intricate work of the goldsmith and jeweller. The inventiveness in design, delicacy of handling, and mastery over hard surfaces, are unsurpassed by anything in the art of the present day. Their successors in the East of the present day retain much of the delicate touch of the cunning workers of ancient times, but their taste for design is usually satisfied with the repetition of the traditional patterns. The metal-worker of to-day uses the same tools in the same way and for the same objects that his forefathers used them. The graving tool, tongs, hammer, anvil, and bellows are found in all, only differing in size and strength as they are applied to iron and copper or gold and silver.

The primitive anvil (Is. xli. 7) is a simple cube inserted in a block of oak-log, and the bellows (Is. liv. 16; Jer. vi. 29) is made of the skin of a goat or cow with the hair left on.

(1) *Iron.*—The smith of the present day makes many things in iron that were formerly made of copper or bronze. The farmer and mason are his chief customers. He is usually engaged in making ploughs, hoes, pick-axes, sickles, horse-shoes, nails, window-bars, and masons' tools. When the Philistines oppressed Israel, iron was made an object of special prohibition (1 Sam. xiii. 19), much in the same way as the Bible has been during the conflict for religious liberty.

(2) *Copper.*—Ordinary copper is chiefly used for cooking utensils, and for the large vessels of the wine-press, olive-press, and also for the preparations of the dyer. They are

hammered into shape out of flat circular plates of the metal. To prevent copper-poisoning these pots are heated over the smith's charcoal fire, and receive a lining of tin, which melts on the hot metal, and is spread by a cloth and sal ammoniac. Tin in the European form does not belong to the East; it is only used for coating copper vessels, and in alloy with copper to make brass, which is called by the

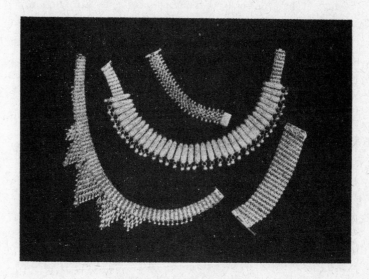

BRACELET AND NECKLACE.

Arabs yellow copper. This is used for more ornamental articles such as trays, ewers, lamps, and vases.

(3) *Gold and silver.*—Silver is of course much more extensively used than gold. It is largely obtained from the head-dress coins and old ornaments of the Bedawîn and peasant women. Refining is done by means of alkalis, and dross and alloy are removed as described in Is. i. 25; Jer. vi. 29; Zech. xiii. 9; Mal. iii. 3.

The commonest forms of ornament are the following: (*a*) *Ear-rings* (Gen. xxxv. 4; Ex. xxxii. 2 · Ezek. xvi. 12).

These are in the form of balls, long pendants, crescents, and discs. The large crescents have a loop that passes over the ear, where it is generally tied to a lock of hair. (b) *Necklaces* (Is. iii. 19). These "chains" are composed of balls, squares, or hollow cylinders of filigree, or are made of massive twist or intricately woven chain-work. The chain on the neck was often a symbol of office (Gen. xli. 42). Neck-bands with crescents attached are still worn on camels (Judges viii. 26). (c) *Finger-rings* (1 Kings xxi. 8). These are often referred to in the Bible. They are not only for ornament with inserted jewels, but also used as signets. These seal-rings are often worn suspended by a cord round the neck. (d) *Bracelets* (Gen. xxiv. 22; Is. iii. 19). These have the same varieties of pattern as the necklaces, thin bangles of gold, silver, brass, and coloured glass being very common. (e) *Armlets* (2 Sam. i. 10). These are of solid twist, or flat bands, with engraved pattern, and sometimes jewelled, clasping the arm by the elasticity of the metal, and leaving an opening of half an inch or more. They are chiefly worn by the Bedawîn, as they still wear the primitive sleeves with long points, which are tied behind the neck when the arm is bared for active exercise. Any ornament upon the arm is thus displayed. (f) *Anklets* (Is. iii. 18) are open rings of plain twist, or with bells and discs attached, now chiefly worn by Bedawîn women. (g) *Nose-rings* (Is. iii. 21; Ezek. xxiii. 25) are confined to the same class, being thin plain rings attached to the centre or wing of the nose. In the Bible the context does not always determine whether the ring mentioned was for the ear or nose, and in such cases the R.V. gives simply "ring." It seems to have been the most primitive of all, and may have first passed into ornamental use as a symbol of religious dedication and a token of guardianship. (h) *Amulets* (Is. iii. 20, R.V.) To the Oriental mind all the above-mentioned ornaments have more or less an amulet value, protecting especially against the evil eye. Some are made solely for this purpose in the shape of silver discs and caskets, but as they are also made of other things they will be referred to in connection with the religious life. (*i*) The work of the goldsmith and silversmith is also required for such church furniture as candlesticks, lamps, censers, and the vessels of Holy Communion.

A TRAY OF BREAD.

5. Bakers.—Among the peasantry and Bedawîn, the baking of bread is one of the chief household duties, but in the towns and principal villages the larger oven of the regular baker is required. The superiority of this bread is implied in the Arabic proverb, which teaches that the best is the cheapest in the end—"Send your bread to the oven of the baker though he should eat the half of it."

The modern Oriental baker does not as a rule prepare the dough, but confines himself to the firing of what is sent to him for that purpose. One of the common sights in an Oriental town is that of the baker's boy carrying on his head a tray of new bread for one house, and on his side a similar tray for another house. The batch is prepared in the house and sent to the baker in the form of round balls of dough, which he kneads into flat cakes for the oven. Jewish women have a custom of taking out a small handful of the dough and rubbing it with earth, or wrapping it in a rag and then laying it beside the dough on the tray so that the baker may throw it into the fire at the side of the oven. It is evidently a relic of sacrificial custom (Lev. vi. 5), and meant to be a token of gratitude to God, but popular superstition gives it another name which in Arabic means "Satan's portion." It is to keep off the evil eye.

The oven.—The Oriental oven is a long, low, stone-built vault, like half a railway-engine's boiler, with a stone pavement down the middle, and a long narrow strip at each side for the firewood. In the evening the ashes are raked out and the children of the poor often bring a piece of tin, or broken water-jar, on which to carry home some of the glowing embers for the cooking of the evening meal (Is. xxx. 14). In the night the brush-wood and logs are laid in position for the baking of the next morning, the door of the oven being closely shut to keep in the heat and prevent the rapid consumption of the fuel. The reference to this in Hosea vii. 4, 6 rather implies that the bakers attended to the preparation of the dough as well as the baking of the loaves. Ancient Jerusalem had its Baker's Street (Jer. xxxvii. 21). Besides the ordinary bread, many kinds of cakes, sweet-meats, and seasoned dishes are baked in these public ovens, especially during the days before and after religious fasts.

6. Apothecaries. — This word is translated "per-fumers" in the Revised Version. The original word includes both meanings, referring to the medicinal value of certain herbs and the essential oils obtained from their flowers and seeds, as well as to their application to cosmetics and the flavouring of food. All large Oriental towns such as Alexandria and Beyrout have their Perfumer's Street. Their stock includes anything fragrant in the form of loose powder, compressed cake, or essences in spirit, oil, or fat, as well as seeds, leaves, and bark.

Such perfumes are mentioned in connection with the holy oil and incense of the tabernacle (Ex. xxx. 5, 35), the rich ritual of Baal-worship (Is. lvii. 9), and the embalming of the dead and the rites of burial (Gen. l. 2; 2 Ch. xvi. 14; Luke xxiii. 56). The smell of incense is perceived on entering an Oriental church, and the smoking censer always accompanies the funeral procession. Orientals are very fond of scents and flavours, some of those they like best, however, being considered heavy and oppressive by Europeans. When the orange-trees, violets, and roses are in blossom, the women make scented waters which they keep in large, closely-sealed bottles for use in summer as cooling syrup-drinks. These are presented to guests in tumblers on brass and silver trays. The king's female "confectionaries" (1 Sam. viii. 13) would be occupied with the preparation and mixing of such flavouring essences. One of the picturesque figures in the streets of an Oriental town in summer, is that of the man who walks up and down with his large leather or glass bottle, selling iced water flavoured with violet essence, rose-water, liquorice, or mastic. He calls out to the idle and the active, among the merchants sitting at their shop doors and the carpenters and blacksmiths busy at their trades, temptingly clapping his brass saucers and cups, and crying "Ho, thou thirsty one! For nothing, for nothing!" The refreshing effect of a cool tumblerful for a farthing makes it seem as if his advertisement was almost true. It is always suggestive of Is. lv. 1.

The enjoyment of perfume is referred to in Prov. xxvii. 9 ; Song of Sol. i. 3. It is especially connected with festivities and crowded gatherings. In the Jewish synagogue, on a warm summer morning, the servant of the congregation sprinkles a little rose-water among the worshippers.

The passage of a carriage occupied by musk-scented Oriental ladies makes a distinct lingering train in the air, like the Gulf Stream in the ocean. Thus Solomon's palanquin with its dust-blown escort filled the air of the wilderness with its rich fragrance (Song of Sol. iii. 6). Certain scents were and still are very costly. Such in its concentrated and purest form is otto of roses, the name being a corruption of the Arabic 'atar—essence, perfume. These perfumes were kept in beautiful vases of translucent alabaster, and the term was applied to any precious vases of similar form although made of metal and other materials. When it is said that the vase was broken (Mark xiv. 3), the reference is to the breaking open of the seal at the top of it. Such scent vases are found in the ancient tombs with something of the scent still clinging to them. The knowledge of the healing virtues of certain herbs was the great contribution of Jewish and Saracen doctors to European medicine.

It is when we understand the higher value set upon these perfumes and essences by Orientals that we realise how much is meant by the words of the Preacher, "A good name is better than precious ointment" (Eccl. vii. 1).

7. Fishermen.—The Bible speaks of the fish of the Nile (Is. xix. 8), and of the sea (Neh. xiii. 16 ; Hos. iv. 3 ; Zeph. i. 3), but the most frequent allusions to the art of fishing are in connection with the Sea of Galilee. These of course are fresh-water fish. The Lake contains vast quantities of them, and the danger of the breaking net

and sinking boat is still at times encountered (Luke v. 6). There are three principal ways of fishing.

(1) *The casting-net.*—When using this, the fisherman stands on the bank or wades breast-deep into the water, and skilfully throws the net which he had arranged on his arm into the water in front of him. It falls in the shape of a ring, and as the lead weights around the fringe drag it down, the net takes the shape of a dome or cone in sinking, and finally falls upon the fishes it encloses. The fisherman then dives down and draws the leads securely together, and carries net and fish to the bank. Favourite spots are the warm springs above Magdala, where the fish congregate in vast swarms, and the fisherman frequently flings in some bait to bring them to one spot, and near enough to the shore for his purpose.

(2) *The drag net* is of the same open form as is used in herring and salmon fishing, with floats along the top and leads along the bottom of the net. It is worked from boats by forming a loop, and thus enclosing the fish.

(3) *Hooks.*—Fishing by the hook or angle is referred to in Is. xix. 8; Am. iv. 2; Hab. i. 15; Matt. xvii. 27. On calm summer nights on the Mediterranean coast fish are speared (Job xli. 7) by a trident, being attracted to the surface by a moving torch held over the stern of the boat.

The application of the fisher's art to the service of the Gospel (Matt. iv. 19) inculcates patience, self-effacement, and the use of appliances in perfect order.

8. **Fowlers and Hunters.**—The chase has always been a favourite pastime wherever a high value has been set on skill, courage, and endurance.

The sculptures of Assyria and the paintings of Egypt portray hunting scenes in which large game is attacked with spears, panthers, and dogs, and smaller game on land and water is caught with snares. The sarcophagi recently discovered at Sidon contain beautiful panels in marble representing hunting scenes. Hunting is frequently referred to in the Psalms and Prophets, and three principal methods are mentioned. These are (1) *shooting with the bow and arrows* (Ex. xxvii. 3), now superseded by the fowling-piece; (2) *snaring* by the spring net (Am. iii. 5) and cage (Jer. v. 27), especially for birds, such as quail, partridge, and duck; (3) pits covered with a net and brush-wood for deer, foxes, wolves, bears, etc. (Ps. xxxv. 7; Is. xxiv. 18, xlii. 22).

Sparrows, linnets, and other small birds are caught by bird-lime set on trees beside a decoy cage. Some are kept as song-birds, but most of them are hung like trout on twigs, a dozen or so in each bunch, and sold for food as cheaply as when Christ taught from their lives the lesson of our heavenly Father's care (Matt. x. 29).

The partridge is not only ever watchful and ready to take flight, but when suddenly come upon it has wonderful confidence in the protective value of its spots. A brood or covey of them will lie motionless, almost at the hunter's feet, without being discovered. David was acquainted with these ways and resources of the bird when he compared the trouble Saul was giving himself to the hunting of the partridge (1 Sam. xxvi. 20).

Serpent charmers are seen from time to time, who entice the snakes from their hiding-places, and make a livelihood by exhibiting them twisting harmlessly around their persons. Usually after a time the man with the snake-bag is missed from his usual rounds, and on inquiry one is told that he died of snake-bite. The Bible refers to the serpent that refuses to be charmed, and makes it an emblem of the deadened conscience (Ps. lviii. 3, 4, 5) and of implacable hatred (Jer. viii. 17).

The moral suggestiveness of the fowler's art turns on the power that evil acquires when concealed behind an

apparent good, the revelry of recovered freedom, the
unexpectedness of calamity, and the vengeance of the
moral law when a man lays a snare for himself (Ps.
cxxiv. 7 ; Eccl. ix. 12 ; Judges viii. 27 ; Pr. xxvi. 27).

9. Day-labourers.—Every Oriental town has a well-
known place where men congregate at dawn and wait to
be engaged in manual labour for the day. Such labour

LABOURERS WAITING AT DAYBREAK.

includes gardening, ditching, repairing walls, white-
washing, and porterage.

The labourer stands either without any tools, or with
the trowel, spade, hoe, or rope that he is accustomed to
use. The common time of engagement is shortly after
sunrise; the unengaged hang about for a few hours and
then generally go elsewhere in search of small jobs. Such
day-labourers are usually too lazy, irregular, or inefficient
to follow a regular trade. They expect to have an over-

seer over them to keep them from loitering, and when the time of payment comes, some incident in the day's proceedings is frequently discovered on which to found a claim for more than the sum agreed upon. The altercation of Matt. xx. 12, from a variety of causes, is often repeated.

These day-labourers live from hand to mouth, and each day's hire is needed at sunset to purchase the family supper, which is always the chief meal of the day (Deut. xxiv. 14, 15).

POTTER'S WHEEL.

10. Pottery.—(1) *Its usefulness.* In the East the expensiveness of copper vessels, the unsuitableness of leather bottles for many of the requirements of town and village life, and the fragility of earthenware, create a large and constant demand for the potter. Earthenware jars are also preferred for holding drinking-water, as the evaporation from the porous substance helps to keep the water cool. In the warm East it is a point of courtesy to give "a cup of *cold* water" (Matt. x. 42).

(2) *The wheel.*—The clay is trodden by the feet until it is reduced to a suitable and uniform consistency. A quantity of it is then lifted and laid on the table beside the potter. He keeps beside him a dish of water into which at any moment he can dip his fingers. The instrument consists of an upright, revolving wooden rod to which two horizontal wooden discs are firmly attached,

ORIENTAL POTTERY.

so that whatever turns one turns the other also. Hence the prophet speaks of the *wheels* of a certain potter (Jer. xviii. 3). The lower and larger one is driven by a spurn of the heel, the upper by a push of the hand. The potter has a considerable variety to choose amongst, even in the shapes and sizes of the common water pitchers, apart from such articles as cooking-pots and jars for olives, cooking-butter, grape-syrup, etc. When during the process of moulding the lump seems to be insufficient or too much for one form, he can convert it into a somewhat different form. To break off or add a fresh lump of clay would involve a fresh commencement. The potter can do what he likes with the clay, but not with himself; he must make the best possible use of each lump. His liberty is directed by wisdom. The form, ornamentation, and to a large extent the colour of the pottery, as drab, red, or black, are determined at the moist stage. The baking makes these unchangeable.

(3) *The baking.*—After being lifted from the wheel the vessel is set on a shelf along with rows of others, where they are all exposed to the wind from every direction, but sheltered from the sun until they are considerably dried and hardened. They are then arranged in the brick-kiln, a shallow well of brickwork or stone about four feet deep and eight or ten feet in diameter, with a small oven of brick at the base. The pottery is piled up over this until the wall rises like a cone to the height of some twelve feet. It is thickly covered with brushwood to keep in the heat and prevent sudden chilling from outside. The fire is kept burning below until the pottery is sufficiently hardened. A few of the jars come out bent at the neck, with a dint in the middle, or a general lean to one side, and the ground around a potter's kiln is always thickly strewn with the broken pieces of the vessels that, in spite of his skill and care, have proved unable to stand the test of fire. The expression "make strong the brick-kiln" (Nah. iii. 14), refers to the reconstruction of the circular wall and the dome when the kiln is to be filled with bricks to be fired.

Besides the uses referred to, clay was the writing-material of Assyria and Babylon. Job refers to the impression produced upon it by the seal or mould, and compares the clay tablet under its relief-design to embroidered cloth (Job xxxviii. 14).

Clay bricks dried in the sun or by fire were extensively used for underground stone houses, cisterns, fortresses, and dwelling - houses. The successive demolitions of Lachish (Tel-el-Hesy), recently explored by the Palestine Exploration Fund, lie like the layers of a Scotch pebble. At the present day in Syria, wherever building-stone is scarce, houses are built of sun-dried brick except on the side or gables facing the western rainy quarter. Hence the reference to the thief as *digging through* the walls of houses (Job xxiv. 16).

(4) *The Scripture illustrations* drawn from pottery emphasise three important resemblances between it and the spiritual life. (*a*) *The subjection of the clay to the potter* (Is. xxix. 16, xlv. 19, lxiv. 8; Jer. xviii. 4-11; Rom. ix. 21). This teaches the possibilities of faith and the iniquity of rebellion against the will of God. An Arabic proverb says, "The potter can put the ear where he likes." (*b*) *Its cheapness and insignificance.*—Hand pitchers cost one halfpenny, and large ones for carrying water from the fountain about twopence. Such is the humiliation of Zion described in Lam. iv. 2. Fervent words from a wicked heart are compared to silver dross over an earthen vessel (Prov. xxvi. 23). The earthen vessel can hold what is valuable without having any value of its own. Such is the condition of Christian grace and the Christian service (2 Cor. iv. 7). (*c*) *Fragility.*—It is very easily broken and cannot be mended. Sometimes a small hole in a jar can be stopped up with mud, rag, or dough, but usually the knock or fall that breaks one part breaks it altogether and instantaneously (Ps. ii. 9, xxxi. 12; Is. xxx. 14; Jer. xix. 11; Rev. ii. 27). This frailty is alluded to in a familiar Arabic proverb which teaches patience amid provocations: "If there were no breakages, there would be no potteries." David speaks of his strength as "dried up like a potsherd" (Ps. xxii. 15). These fragments lie

about everywhere, exposed to all kinds of weather, and
are practically indestructible. Archæologists tell us that
they often render very important service. The sorrows
of God's people have been as helpful as their songs.

11. Hewers of wood and Drawers of water (Deut.
xxix. 11 ; Joshua ix. 21).—These are still among the
humblest occupations in the land. Timber is scarce all
over western Palestine, especially in Judæa. Charcoal
burners go up to the mountains where oak and pine trees
may still be met with, but the hewer of wood is generally
content to glean among trees and tree-roots left in less
remote localities. It is one of the common sights in
Jerusalem to see the small load of twigs and roots, chiefly
of old olive-trees, being brought in for sale on a man's
back or that of his donkey. It involves so much toil and
time, and is so poorly paid, that only the poorest and
those unskilled in labour attempt to gain a living in this
way. Similarly the drawer of water, who brings water
from the fountain and carries it to the houses, often has a
long way to go, and a long time to wait before his turn
comes round to fill his jars or skins. It is generally a
feeble old man who now does it, and the water is carried
on the back of a donkey too old and infirm to keep pace
with the other baggage - animals. Jeremiah mentions
among the sorrows of Israel in its days of humiliation,
that the young men were made to do donkey's and mule's
work in turning mill-wheels, and the children were set to
carry wood, and often stumbled under loads that were too
heavy for them (Lam. v. 13).

12. Tax - gatherers. — The publicans of the Roman
Empire are represented by a numerous and flourishing
class in the modern East. The farming out of import and
export duties, excise on tobacco, salt, etc., and of the
Government tithe on produce, is universally practised. A
commercial company guarantees to the Government a fixed

sum for a certain tax or monopoly, and then directly or by further sub-letting proceeds to fix such a scale of charges as will ensure a profit by the transaction. It leads to much oppression and injustice, and fosters a feeling of hostility towards anything connected with the Government. Through long continuance it has ceased to be regarded as a social wrong. The public conscience accepts it as a necessity; and in a Turkish custom-house men may be met with of the type of Zacchæus, with honest instincts and even spiritual desires (Luke xix. 23).

13. **Money-changers.** — The work of the money-changers is twofold, namely, to change money from one kind of currency to another, and to give change in the same currency. He charges about twopence for changing a pound, and the change received has always to be carefully scrutinised, both as to quantity and quality. At times they systematically keep a small, useful coin out of circulation, until its scarcity increases its value by a farthing or more, and then let it return to the shops. These small profits to them are a great inconvenience to the public.

The money-changer sits all day at the street corner with his little box in front of him, occasionally clinking his coins to advertise his presence. The variety of coinage in Syria and Palestine is exceedingly perplexing to those recently arrived in the country. In a church collection there may be found, besides ordinary Turkish coins, francs and half-francs of Austria, France, and Italy, with copper and silver coins from England and India.

In ancient Jerusalem the presence of worshippers from the different lands of their commercial residence and political dispersion must have brought many different coins into circulation (Acts ii. 9, 10, 11). In the time of Christ, a custom begun for the convenience of strangers

and the general public had become a mercenary scandal
in the temple, and the money-changers were expelled
with the others who had converted the house of prayer
into a noisy Oriental bazaar (Matt. xxi. 12).

14. Bankers.—Small sums of money are frequently
lent and borrowed among Orientals on the strength of
friendship and kinship. Very often they remain unpaid,
and this light treatment of a promise within a privileged
circle of relationship is easily extended to ordinary business
engagements. When money is advanced, or goods are
forwarded to a merchant on the guarantee of a mutual
friend, if some plausible excuse can be found for non-fulfil-
ment of contract, the mere breaking of one's word is not
regarded as disgraceful. The unforeseen obstacle is interpreted as something sent from above, and to be
accepted with pious submission ! The party imposed
upon has no tribunal of business honour or public opinion
to appeal to by which the defaulter might be put to shame
and inconvenience, and prosecution would likely lead to a
competition in legal bribery. The loser feels that his
business capacity has been discredited by the transaction,
and expatiates to sympathetic friends on the cleverness with
which he has been duped (Luke xvi. 8). Notwithstanding
such drawbacks, which are due to general want of veracity
and of moral tone, rather than to a purpose of deliberate
villainy, the practice of lending out money at interest is
widespread and popular. Servant-girls loan out their
earnings in petty usury. Syrian cabmen were among the
sufferers by the recent depreciation of South African mine-
shares. Many of the wealthy Syrian Christians made
their money by mortgaging the lands of the Egyptian
peasantry under the *régime* of the old Khedives, and
bitterly lament the interference caused by the British
occupation of that country. Among the Moslems the
taking of interest is prohibited by the Koran as unbrotherly

and inhuman, but ways of evasion are easily found. The common charge is about one per cent per month, but this is often exceeded. The Jewish money-lender who wins an ugly notoriety in Christian lands of the West is only walking in the steps of Oriental tradition. When an Oriental Christian shows signs of independent thought and a spirit of religious inquiry, it is a common device of the monks to find some way of lending him money, after the manner of a friendly Shylock, and when he is unable to repay it, to screw him into dutiful submission to the Church. For the past two hundred years Armenians have been the leading money-changers, bankers, and tax-gatherers of the East, and the hatred thus accumulated by a few was one of the chief incentives to the persecution that recently destroyed so many of their innocent and helpless countrymen. Usury and deceit are among the chief causes that make Oriental Christianity weak and contemptible in the presence of Islam.

Such are some of the colours that have to be put on the palette when *the rich man of Scripture* sits for his portrait.

15. Merchants.—The Bible references to merchandise are chiefly to the trading caravans of the overland route passing east and west, north and south, through the Promised Land. Their halting-stations at such places as Palmyra and Jerash are marked by broken pillars, amphi-theatres, and general desolation, for their merchandise is now with the trade-carrying nation that rules the sea. They are now poorly represented by the travelling pedlar with the box or bundle of wares on his back : their profits and practices are found in the bazaar-shops of the Oriental towns and villages.

(1) *Shops.*—A collection of small shops in a square or in rows of streets is called the Bazaar. The goods of the travelling merchant used to be stored in a khan, or large

building, composed of a number of rooms built round an open square, and in charge of a keeper. Here the commodities were exposed for sale during the day and guarded during the night. The open city square or row of shops under the protection of city police is an expansion of this. The shop is a small room without windows, whose whole front opens on the street. There the shopkeeper sits, and passers-by see all that is exposed for sale.

(2) *Weights.*—When the goods are sold by the piece or by length a standard measure properly marked is used, but when by weight the customer is very much at the mercy of the merchant. The weights are very often mere lumps of black stone, broken chain-links, or irregular small blocks of iron. Probably the merchant in ancient times had the same facilities for cheating (Prov. xi. 1, xvi. 11, xx. 10).

(3) *The price.*—This in common Oriental usage is determined partly by the value of the article and partly by the appearance of the customer. A few shops invite Europeans by a placard of "fixed price," but on nearer approach this usually fades into an aspiration. A fair price is described as one that is "good for the wolf and good for the sheep."

Several other trades, handicrafts, and manufactures remain to be referred to briefly, or noticed afterwards in other connections : *Soap,* in which mineral or vegetable alkali and olive oil are used in the composition, is made in several places, that of Tripoli and Haifa being especially esteemed. *The tanning of hides* for leather bottles, harness, and shoes, and for export in the raw condition, is an industry at most large towns, and extensively at Jaffa (Joppa) and Hebron, at which latter place glass vessels and ornaments are also manufactured. The *butcher* among the Jews is a kind of ecclesiastic, who exercises official censorship at the slaughter-house, extracts the prohibited sinew

(Gen. xxxii. 32), and kills fowls in the proper way with the proper knife, especially the sacrificial white fowls for the Day of Atonement. Some of these customs seem to us rather odd and antiquated, but they served a sanitary purpose in the past, and it is still especially safe to purchase meat in the shop of an Oriental Jewish butcher. *Millers* will be spoken of in connection with the domestic hand-mill, the *door-keeper* with the house, the *forerunner* with travel, the *letter-writer* and *teacher* with education, and *law* and *medicine* along with property and religion.

CHAPTER V

DOMESTIC LIFE AND FAMILY RELATIONSHIPS

The owner of a house knows what is in it.
The garment of peace never fades.
Birth is the messenger of death.—*Syrian Proverbs*.

HAVING seen the shepherd with his sheep, the farmer in his fields, and the tradesmen at their different labours, we shall now notice the family life for the sake of which those occupations exist.

We shall first inspect the house and its arrangements, the preparation of food and the table customs, the different articles and styles of dress, and so pass to the chief relationships and incidents of family life. We shall then be prepared in a concluding chapter to observe how the conditions and customs we have been studying are repeated and expanded in public affairs, giving its peculiar character to the social, political, and religious life of the East.

1. The House.—As in other lands, the house is a place of privacy and protection against cold, but in the East it is very specially a place of shelter from the heat. There are traces here and there of the caves in which pre-historic man dwelt, and shepherds take their sheep to similar caves; they were the retreats of fugitives in times of oppression in Israel, and at the present day the deserted stone dens of Bashan and the rock-cut cells of Christian monks show this primitive cave-type of architecture.

(1) *The tent.*—This is the simplest form of dwelling in general use, and is characteristic of the Bedawîn class or wandering shepherds. It is a low covering of black goat's hair, with its open front kept up by two poles. This opening may be regarded as the original of all doors, and reached its largest and most beautiful form in the gates of the cities, and of the temple at Jerusalem. The tent is held in position by ropes of the same material tied

SHEPHERD'S TENT.

to rough oak pegs driven into the ground by a mallet (Judges iv. 21, v. 26). A curtain hangs down in the middle, separating the women's apartment from the public room. While thus screened from view the women can easily hear what is being said in the public room or at the door of the tent (Gen. xviii. 10), and can look out through the cane-lattice.

The tent remained in use after Israel had largely settled down to agriculture It was the emblem of a simple, unfettered life, and when any national measure was to be rejected, the cry was raised, "To your tents, O Israel"

(2 Sam. xx. 1 ; 1 Kings xii. 16). The dignity of ancestral associations gave the tent a place above the stone-built house in the language of poetry and prophecy (Ps. lxxxiv. 1-10 ; Song of Songs i. 5 ; Jer. iv. 20). At the present day those who are brought up in the tent are very reluctant to leave it. It is socially a degradation in their eyes, and personally a sacrifice of preference. A few years ago the young wife of a Bedawi sheikh in Damascus died of longing for the life she had left behind her. Her husband had been previously married to an English lady of aristocratic family, who used to live part of the year with him in the desert, and the rest of the year he lived with her in Damascus, where she had adorned the house with many articles of taste and beauty, and laid out the garden with a choice variety of plants and flowering shrubs. When she died the sheikh married a young princess of his own people and took her to his city house. In a very short time she began to lose health and spirits, and though her husband bought for her beautiful dresses and jewellery, and Oriental ladies visited her and invited her to their houses, she drooped and died. Her heart was with the gatherings around the well, the camels and kids about the tent, and all the simple free life of the wilderness.

In Jer. xxxv. 2-7 the obedience of the Rechabites to a family vow is contrasted with the unfaithfulness of Israel in departing from the commandments of God.

(2) *Houses of the village and town.*—The ordinary house of the peasant often consists of one room. The Arabic word for a house also means a room, and doubtless it was so among the ancient Hebrews. In the middle of the room a wooden or stone pillar supports the large cross beam of the flat roof, and on this pillar there is usually a small shelf for the oil lamp, which thus gives light to all in the room or house (Matt. v. 15).

If the house is to contain two rooms they are not built

side by side, but with the breadth of a room left between them. Between the ends a wall is built connecting the two rooms, and the house has thus its open court.

If the house is to have three rooms, a room takes the place of the wall at the end of the court. If more than three rooms are needed, additions are made to those at the side, thus increasing the length of the court. For a large family of the wealthy class, where the grand-parents have

ORIENTAL HOUSE.

several married sons staying with them, there may be several courts leading into one another with rooms around each, set apart for the several households. The rooms do not usually communicate with each other, but have their doors opening into the court. As a protection against sun and rain a roofed colonnade often runs round the area, or a verandah projects from the wall. In a small house of one or two rooms an awning of leaves and brush-wood or of old boarding casts its shade over the door, or partly covers the court to protect the entrance to the

room at the end of it. This must have been the part of
the roof removed when the sick of the palsy was lowered
and laid at the feet of Christ (Mark ii. 4).

(3) *The roof.*—This is composed of one or more large
logs laid across, with small pieces resting upon them.
The whole is covered with a layer of broom, heath, and
reeds, and upon this earth is spread to a thickness of several
inches. When this has been trodden, rolled, and pressed
down, the surface of the flat roof is finally made water-
proof with a coating of lime or cement, with openings in
the low parapet wall by which the rain may flow off.

(4) This *battlement-wall* (Deut. xxii. 8) is not so carefully attended to as it used to be, and the want of this
precaution is a frequent cause of accident. Corner pieces
are built about six feet high, and clothes-lines are stretched
between them. In Moslem houses the spaces between these
corner pillars are often filled in with boards or perforated
brick-work, so that the roof may be resorted to by the
family without their being seen by their neighbours.

It is regarded as unneighbourly for men to walk about
on the roof, as they might look down into the open courts
of other houses. Among the peasantry one of the chief
uses of the roof is for the drying of grain, summer fruits,
and fuel for winter use (Josh. ii. 6).

Village proclamations are made from the roof, and at
marriages it is often a place of assemblage, where the
guests sing songs and keep up a rhythmic stamping and
clapping of hands (Judges xvi. 27).

(5) *The upper room* (2 Kings ii. 1, xxiii. 12; Mark
xiv. 15; Acts i. 13, ix. 37, xx. 8).—This is a familiar
feature of Oriental houses. It is an adaptation to the
climate. In summer, booths or arbours of leaves and
branches are put up as sleeping-places for greater coolness
at night. The upper room is the same in a permanent
form. Where several rooms were thus built on the roof

it became what the Bible calls *the summer house* as contrasted with *the winter house* downstairs (Judges iii. 20 ; Jer. xxxvi. 22 ; Amos iii. 15). A similar change is effected in large houses by occupying the eastern side in winter and the western in summer. The roof is reached by a rough wooden ladder, or flight of stone steps, passing up the outside wall of the house, or along one of the walls of the court. The upper room, as a place of quiet retreat and refreshing coolness, is usually better built and furnished than the ordinary rooms, and a guest spending the night, as distinguished from a mere visitor, is accommodated there. The room on the wall built for the man of God (2 Kings iv. 10) was meant to be a place of retirement in keeping with his sacred office and habits of prayer.

(6) *The guest-room.*—Orientals do not usually set apart a room for a guest, as this would be considered discourtesy almost amounting to dismissal. Orientals dislike being left alone, and at night prefer to have a small light in the room. As they sleep with their clothes on there is not the same need for privacy, and if the bed for a guest be spread in the upper room, some of the sons of the family usually have theirs spread beside his for the sake of companionship. An Oriental feels himself deserted when *made at home* in a European family, and conversely, a European finds himself oppressed by the constant presence and attentions of his Oriental host.

The ordinary guest-room for the reception of casual visitors in small houses is the room at the end of the court. It is usually more open than the other family rooms of the house. It corresponds to the raised divan at the end of the one-roomed house as the place of honour to which guests are conducted. In larger houses a specially large and well-furnished room is assigned for this purpose conveniently near the door, so that visitors may not be kept waiting, and that the family may be disturbed as little as possible.　As refreshment is usually offered to guests, the guest-room is also *the banqueting-hall.*

(7) *The floor.*—Wooden floors are rarely seen.　In villages the usual floor is of mud pressed down by wooden stamps, and rubbed smooth by a large flat pebble ; a more cleanly and durable form is that of cement composed of lime and small pebbles stamped down in the same way ; the best floor is of square slabs of limestone.　In good town houses the public rooms are paved with white marble relieved by bands of black slate, or designs in marble of different colours.　Large open courts are often paved in this way, with an ornamental marble fountain in the centre, and spaces are left in the pavement for orange, lemon, and other fragrant evergreen trees and shrubs.

(8) *Furnishing and ornament.*—The *walls* are usually of plaster coated with a wash of lime, but in the houses of the rich, especially in Damascus, the walls of the more public rooms are adorned with beautiful mosaic of wood, marble, mother-of-pearl, crystal, and ivory.　The decoration is usually in the form of intricate geometrical designs, but flowers and animals are occasionally introduced.　Swords, daggers, and guns often adorn the walls.　There is no attempt at wall-paper, or desire for the small busy patterns stamped upon them.　The warm climate, with its relaxing influence, creates a demand for the restfulness of blank spaces.　In the richly adorned reception-rooms there is little to suggest the harmonious surroundings of a cultivated mind.　The impression is not of something needed and naturally enjoyed by the owner in his beautiful home, but of something that a rich man wants to announce to his visitors.　Beautiful carpets of wool, camel-hair, and silk lie on the marble floor ; a divan runs round three sides of the room, the cushions having coverings of cotton, wool, silk, and gold thread from the native looms.　These, with a large mirror at one end of the room, a glass

candelabrum suspended from the roof, and a marble fountain sometimes placed below it, with a few small inlaid tables here and there, are the usual ornaments of the Eastern drawing-room.

(9) *Doors.*—The door is a place of peculiar sanctity and importance. The difference between the outside and inside is that of two different worlds. In large houses the door-keeper sits at the entrance to answer inquiries and conduct visitors within, and at night he sleeps in a small room within the entrance at the side of the door, keeping guard over the premises. He corresponds to the watchman of the city-gate and the vineyards. He is charged with the protection of the family without being included in its membership, and after conducting guests to the door retires to his post of duty. This menial and external position of the door-keeper is alluded to in Ps. lxxxiv. 10.

In smaller houses that have no door-keeper, a servant or member of the family looks over the balcony, or calls out "Who?" If the visitor be one of the family, he answers "Open!" If he be a well-known friend he exclaims "I!" The recognised tone of the voice is sufficient (Acts xii. 13).

(10) *Windows.*—Window-panes of glass are a recent introduction. The usual Oriental window has wooden bars for protection against intrusion and theft, while a frame of lattice screens the lower half of the window, so that those within may look out without being seen. At night windows are closed with wooden shutters, chiefly for privacy and safety, and partly to ward off the light and heat of the sun in the early morning. Hence the allusion to the *opening* of the windows in Mal. iii. 10. In upper rooms the bars are not needed, as they are above the reach of passers-by ; hence the possibility of such incidents as those alluded to in Josh. ii. 15 ; 1 Sam. xix. 12 ; Acts

xx. 9.   In the houses of the city windows do not usually look out upon the street, but in the upper stories balconies often project over the street, with windows commanding a view, and receiving a current of air from either side. In these the lattice-work is frequently of a highly ornamental character. Pitchers of water for drinking are placed beside such windows to be kept cool by the draught

LATTICED WINDOW.

of air. From this circumstance such ornamental lattice-work is called *mashrabîyeh*, from the Arabic *mashrab*, a place for drinking. It is sometimes seen in English drawing-rooms as an artistic screen, without any connection with its original use.

The mother of Sisera is described as looking anxiously from such a window waiting for the son who never returned (Judges v. 28).

Over city gates, and the entrance to fortresses, a small window is placed in the wall or the watch-turret from which any one approaching could be seen without danger to the observer.

(11) *Sleeping arrangements.*—Orientals assemble rather than retire to rest. Thus the father in the parable (Luke xi. 7) pleads that his children are with him, sleeping on their mattresses on the floor around him. When the time for sleep arrives the bedding materials are taken out of the wardrobe, box, or recess in the wall where they have been lying rolled up during the day. Each mattress is stuffed with cotton or wool, and has belonging to it a thick quilt covered with coloured calico or silk, and sewn in longitudinal or diagonal stripes. During sleep an Oriental covers the head as well as the rest of the body with the quilt. It belongs to the sanctities of Oriental life not to disturb sleep or interrupt a meal. It is with the greatest difficulty that a Syrian servant can be got to awake his master at an early hour. When a Moslem has to arouse a fellow-believer from sleep he does so by calling to him, " *God is one !* " The statement of this supreme truth is always in season to the believer, and only an infidel could object to its utterance !

2. Food. 1. *Bread.* — The chief article of food is bread, and the chief work of the house among the peasantry and working classes of the towns is its preparation.

(i.) *Cleansing.*—When brought from the threshing-floor the wheat is carefully and skilfully sifted (Is. xxx. 28 ; Amos ix. 9 ; Luke xxii. 31), in order to remove small stones and particles of clay, and especially to shake out the small poisonous seeds, translated cockle, darnel, and tares, which abound in thorny, neglected fields (Matt. xiii. 7). The prayer for Peter was that his faith might not be tossed aside among the refuse.

The wheat is then washed to purify it from any dust clinging to it, and is dried on sheets spread upon the

house-top. It is then stored for family use in the house
in large churn-like barrels made of wicker-work and clay,
with an opening near the foot by which the quantity
required at a time may be taken out. Larger quantities,
to be kept for flour or next season's sowing, are stored in
underground cisterns or dry wells with narrow openings,
which are carefully covered over so that only the owners
may know where the cistern is.

(ii.) *Grinding.*—When wheat or barley is ground for

HAND-MILL.

the market it is sent to the mill, which in some places
works all the year round, but usually only in winter, when
there is a sufficient supply of water to turn the wheel.

The *hand-mill* consists of two circular stones about a foot
and a half in diameter, the lower often with a slightly
convex surface, and the upper hollowed out to fit it. The
lower is made of limestone or basalt, and being thicker is
the heavier of the two ; the upper is made of porous lava-
stone, so that the surface may not become polished by the
friction. On one side, near the circumference, it has a
wooden peg which the two women hold each with a hand
upon it as they sit on opposite sides and grind the wheat.

A pivot rises from the centre of the lower stone, and is inserted in an opening in the centre of the upper one, thus keeping it in its place.   The turning of the hand-mill is referred to in Ex. xi. 5; Judges xvi. 21; Lam. v. 13; Matt. xxiv. 41.   It was forbidden to keep it as a pledge (Deut. xxiv. 6), and to do so is still considered disgraceful. The hardness of the lower stone is alluded to in Job xli. 24.   The removal of the millstone is one of the forfeitures of captive Israel (Jer. xxv. 10); the cessation of the cheerful sound is one of the vanished pleasures in Eccl. xii. 3, 4.

Oriental bread resembles our morning rolls, oat-cakes, and pancakes.   It is not made in large loaves to be cut with a knife, but is torn or broken by the hand (Matt. xxvi. 26; 1 Cor. xi. 24).

(iii.) *Baking* in the family is chiefly done in three ways.

(*a*) Cakes of dough are laid on hot ashes or heated stones (Gen. xviii. 16; Ex. xii. 39; 1 Kings xvii. 12, xix. 6; John xxi. 9).   This is the most primitive way, and comes nearest to the singed or parched corn in the ear, eaten at harvest time before the grain is hard (Josh. v. 11; Ruth ii. 14).   Wheat, after being steeped in water, is sometimes put in cauldrons over a fire until it is thoroughly dried.   It is then loosely ground like very coarse oatmeal, or what is called cracked-wheat.   A kind of porridge is made of it, and it is often cooked along with lentils.   As it is mentioned along with lentils in 2 Sam. xvii. 28, it was probably one of the *parched* preparations in Barzillai's gifts to David.   When finely ground it is the familiar home grocery called semolina, which is also used in most Oriental cakes and sweetmeats.

(*b*) A simple oven is made by putting fuel, generally grass, thorns, and small twigs, into a large earthenware jar, and when the jar is sufficiently heated thin cakes are laid on the outside of it.   More frequently a hole is made in the ground and plastered round, and into it the same kind of fuel is put, along with a few large pebbles to retain the heat. When the smoke and flame have left a glow of hot embers, large thin cakes are slapped upon the sides, and are fired in a minute or two.

(c) A convex griddle, such as is used for oat-cakes, is put over an open-air fire between two stones, and thin cakes are baked on it.

(iv.) *Cakes.*—Various kinds of bread and cakes are made by these simple contrivances, and in the baker's oven already described. Many of them resemble those of the Egyptian monuments, and are suggested by some of the descriptive terms in the Bible. There are crisp network discs covered with sesame seed, paste-buns filled with pounded nuts and folded in triangular shape; threads of vermicelli are twisted together to the thickness of a rope, steeped in a sauce of honey and nuts, and arranged in a flat coil to make a large cake on a flat tray; thin wafers are coated with grape-syrup and powdered with pungent or fragrant seeds and leaf dust; common loaves before being sent to the oven sometimes have the surface rubbed with oil and covered with aromatic seeds, and cakes are occasionally soaked or fried in boiling oil. Thin cakes of unleavened bread, often prepared with whimsical precautions against any contact with leaven, are eaten by the Jews during passover-week (Ex. xvi. 31; Lev. vi. 21, vii. 12; 1 Chron. xxiii. 29).

2. *Water.*—This is next in importance to bread. Orientals drink a great deal of water both at meals and at other times. When sitting at food the small hand-pitcher is constantly passed round. They are able to drink from the mouth or small spout of the jar without touching it with their lips. It belongs to the etiquette of Oriental water-drinking to be careful, in this matter, of the feelings of others. A Persian Moslem regards a pitcher touched by

the lips of a Christian as defiled, and instantly throws it to the ground. Orientals distinguish between different kinds of water to an extent unknown in the West. In a town with several public fountains, they can tell very decisively from which the water in the pitcher has been taken. The water-carrier does not attempt to impose upon those whom he serves. Beggars at the door often ask for water. The demand of the Israelites for water would be a specially imperative one. The pitcher is set within reach at the bedside at night, and Saul's cruse would be missed in the morning as much as his spear (1 Sam. xxvi. 11). When David longed for the water of the well of Bethlehem (2 Sam. xxiii. 15), it was not only because of its association with happy untroubled days, but because he had a distinct remembrance of its peculiar taste. Thus an Arabic proverb sums up the comforts of the prosperous and contented man by saying, "His bread is baked, and his jar is full."

Israel's double condemnation is stated in terms of the vital need and refreshing effect of water (Jer. ii. 13, 18). See also Numb. xxiii. 5 ; 1 Kings xiii. 8, xvii. 10, xix. 6 ; Prov. xxv. 25 ; Is. xxx. 16 ; Am. viii. 11 ; Matt. v. 6, x. 42.

3. *Meat, fish, milk, and fruits.*—One of the commonest family dishes is made of cut pieces of meat stewed with vegetables, such as beans, tomatoes, vegetable marrow, and many others. It is put into a dish, and each one helps himself by making a spoon or small scoop out of a piece of bread freshly torn from the thin loaf at his side By practice this is done with much cleanliness and expertness. When one prepares such a mouthful and hands it to another at table, it is an assurance of friendly regard (John xiii. 26). A lamb or kid is sometimes stewed in milk. The dish is called by the Arabs *mother's milk*, and when it is eaten some apologetic allusion is generally made to the ancient rule against it (Ex. xxiii. 19). At an

Oriental feast a lamb or kid is frequently roasted entire, with the head and legs drawn together and the inside stuffed with rice and seasoning, the whole being served on a large tray. The meat is so thoroughly cooked that it separates easily from the bone, and is lifted off by the fingers in such portions as each one wants to eat. As with the sop, so with this dish, the sheikh or head of the house occasionally lifts off a choice morsel and presents it to one of his guests as a token of affectionate interest and regard.

The Hebrew word for food is *teref*, something snatched or plucked, and evidently originating in this custom of eating with the fingers.

The national dish of Syria is a compound of minced meat and roughly-ground wheat, pounded together in a mortar along with suitable seasoning, until all is reduced to a uniform consistency. It is then spread about an inch thick in a shallow pan, marked off by a knife into diamond-shaped sections, covered with the native cooking butter, and sent to the oven to be baked. Something of this kind seems to be referred to in Prov. xxvii. 22, when it is said that a man of coarse, defiant selfishness will not lose his individuality even after he has been wrought upon in this way by trial and adversity.

Another of the most savoury dishes of the East is that which had such fatal influence upon Esau (Gen. xxv. 34). Lentils are soaked and boiled in as much water as they will absorb. Small parings of onion are fried in oil till they are slightly singed, and added. Cracked-wheat or rice is often cooked along with the lentils. When it is being cooked the smell is very demonstrative, and its appetising relish always makes a very strong appeal to the hungry.

Orientals are not accustomed to make soups: when meat is boiled the water is reduced to a strong sauce to be eaten with the meat. Such were the seething and boiling referred to in Scripture.

Fowls are served roasted and stewed. An Arabic proverb follows the thought of Prov. xv. 17 in saying, " Better to have bread and an onion with peace than stuffed fowl with strife."

In the East the pig is heard rather than seen. The name is constantly on the lips as a term of contempt and abuse, but the flesh is only eaten occasionally by Christians. Unless its food be specially attended to, the scavenger habits of the animal, and the careless ways of the people with regard to refuse, make pig's-flesh an article of food to be prohibited and avoided in this warm country. Even in connection with the flesh of the wild boar fatal outbreaks of trichinosis or pig-worm sometimes occur.

Native Christians occasionally eat the raw flesh of sheep and goats. On the other hand, from a scrupulous desire to remove all the blood, the Jews rub salt into meat before it is cooked.

Fish is abundant in the Mediterranean and the Sea of Galilee, but the Government tax on its sale is prohibitive, and the permissive use of it on Friday among the Oriental Christians causes it to be regarded as inferior and suggestive of penance.

Milk, besides being used in its fresh state, is generally made into a curd-and-whey form either by rennet or by a similar fermentation that gives it a taste of cool sourness. Most likely it was in this last form that Jael gave refreshment to Sisera (Judges iv. 19, v. 25).

Cream is rocked in skins until butter is formed, and this on being boiled is made into cooking-butter, which is stored in jars and used for cooking purposes throughout the year. It is mentioned in books of Arabic travel as saman or samăni, and in India is called ghee. Cheese in its different stages of preparation is constantly used. (1 Sam. xvii. 18).

Salads and relishes are made of cress, lettuce, endive, mallows, mint, cucumber, and many other things. Vegetables of all kinds are largely used, and Orientals have much skill and economical resource in preparing sour, pungent, and aromatic sauces. At the Passover feast the Jews have a sauce that resembles thin lime or liquid chalk in appearance. They dip their bitter leaves of wild endive or dandelion into it as a memorial of the Egyptian bondage.

Fresh fruits are eaten in their season, grapes and oranges lasting longest; eaten with bread they make the meal of a labouring man. Figs, raisins, walnuts, almonds, and pistachio nuts, are the commonest dried fruits (Gen. xliii. 11 ; 1 Sam. xxv. 18).

Locusts are mentioned as the food of John the Baptist; they are used as a poor kind of food by the Arabs of the southern desert, the hind legs of the locust being plucked off and pickled.

4. The chief *meal-time* is a little after sunset. Rest of mind and body are regarded by Orientals as necessary to the enjoyment of food, and the condition of being refreshed and strengthened by it. This means that the duties of the day must be over. Farmers work in fields at some distance from the village, and tradesmen live on the outskirts of the city, and these cannot well come home to a meal at mid-day. Also as the warmth of the climate seldom allows of meat being kept for any time in the house, each day brings its own marketing, so that for men and women the evening meal is the time of family reunion and refreshment. Cushions are taken from the divan and placed around the tray that rests on a small low table. Bread is eaten with everything, at all stages of the meal. Each guest or member of the family has a few thin loaves laid beside him, three being a common number.

For the reason mentioned, all the cooked food is usually eaten at the evening dinner. A proverb says, " The evening guest gets no supper." He may claim shelter and rest at all times, but coming unannounced after supper-time he has no claim on the law of hospitality for food. But Oriental courtesy always considers it better to disturb a neighbour than to disappoint a stranger (Luke xi. 5).

When at a large feast all cannot be accommodated at one time, they seat themselves round the table in relays, each party rising when finished with a salaam of thanks to the host and making room for another.

At family meals the women of the household are the usual attendants; among the wealthier classes servants wait upon the family and its guests. Ordinary domestic servants are chiefly found among Europeans or those Orientals who have adopted their ways.

Originally such service in the higher families of the land was rendered by poor relatives, who received in return occasional gratuities, or by slaves obtained in war or purchased in the market. The taint of such old associations is seen in the reluctance of parents to let their daughters enter service, and in the frequent non-payment of the servant's wages. When a company of Orientals are to enter a room one by one, or take their seats on a divan or at table, considerable attention has to be given to the competing claims of seniority, family dignity, and official position. Some little time is usually spent in protests of self-abasement, each esteeming the other better than himself. Among the Jews a man instructed in the law, although poor in worldly goods, is considered superior to a rich man who has little religious position. It is the reverence of heart towards God's service which the Pharisees accepted and abused when they claimed for themselves the place of honour at social and religious assemblies. An Arabic proverb expresses the thought of Luke xiv. 10, by saying, "Never sit in the place of the man who can say to you, 'Rise.'" As an act of respect the master of the house sometimes attends personally on his guest.

After the meal the hands are washed in the usual

ORIENTAL EWER AND BASIN.

Oriental way, by having water poured over them by one holding a brass ewer. Servants render this office to guests and, at ordinary times, the members of the family do it for each other. The custom is alluded to in 1 Kings iii. 11.

3. **Dress.**—Oriental dress differs from ours with regard

to material, shape, and colour. The commonest material is cotton, either white or dyed indigo-blue; silk, however, being largely used for the outer cloak of women, and wool for that of men. Orientals prefer a long continuous robe covering the body to a costume made up of several smaller articles. Men and women also wear brighter colours than we are accustomed at the present day to see at home. The warmth of the climate is the chief explanation of this preference for light, unconfined, and brightly-coloured costume.

The love of ornament also plays an important part in Oriental dress. The long flowing robes give a heightened appearance to the stature, and the different articles, especially the various styles of the outer cloak, indicate distinctions of social rank.

These are forfeited when the European form of dress is adopted, but, on the other hand, a connection with higher culture and civilisation is thus implied. It is considered that, owing to the recent introduction of European customs and manufactures, a greater change has come over the dress of the people of Syria during the present generation than during the previous thousand years. The transition stage is sometimes trying to both Eastern and Western good taste. A lady has her dress made in the latest European style, but the colour chosen is of Oriental brightness: in the same way a man wearing a European overcoat thinks it more decorative to throw it loosely over the shoulders like an Oriental cloak, leaving the empty sleeves dangling at each side.

The original articles of Oriental dress are the under-shirt and the outer cloak. These two garments are still the ordinary outfit of the Bedawîn. Modifications of these and additions to them were due to the more civilised life of the villages and towns and to contact with other nations. A short description of these as at present worn

in Syria will help us to understand the literal and
figurative references to clothing in the Bible.

(1) *The shirt, sheet, linen garment* (Judges xiv. 12;
Prov. xxx. 24 (R.V.); Is. iii. 23; Mark xiv. 51).—The
people of Palestine, and still more their neighbours in
the warmer climate of Egypt, sometimes cover the body
quite effectively and picturesquely by means of a large
cotton sheet or woollen blanket. It is wound round the
figure with an end thrown loosely over the shoulder. It
is very characteristic of Oriental preference in matters of
dress : they dislike knots, pins, and brooches, in fact,
anything by which their clothing would be firmly and
finally fixed. In a warm climate anything close-fitting
and immovable causes perspiration and discomfort.
The under-shirt is commonly made in a very simple
manner. A long width of cotton is folded into two equal
parts ; the sides are sewn up, with the exception of two
holes at the top corner for the arms ; an opening for the
head and neck completes the dress. When sleeves are
worn they reach nearly to the wrist, with long points
hanging down a little lower than the knee. These
apparent impediments are really conveniences, because
when men are engaged in fighting or active employment, and when the women are busy milking, sweeping,
or grinding, the sleeves are drawn up and kept up by
having the long points tied behind the neck. This
became emblematic of activity, as when the prophet says,
"The Lord hath made bare His holy arm (Is. lii. 10).

Sometimes the neck-opening and the lower parts of the
front are ornamented with coloured needlework of black,
yellow, green, and red silk, as this part is visible when
the only garment over it is the large shepherd cloak.
When another garment is worn between these two the
under-shirt is of plain cotton. It is usually fastened with
a belt when only the cloak is worn over it. When men

are engaged in summer in such work as sawing timber, fishing, or treading clay for the potter, the under dress is merely a cloth fastened round the waist and reaching to the knees. In any case, whether the under garment be large or small, a man wearing this only is said to be naked or undressed (John xxi. 7).

(2) *Cloak.*—This is the outside garment proper, and is not usually bound with a girdle. It is the outer coat of

CLOAK AND EMBROIDERED SHIRT.

the Eastern traveller and shepherd. The broad black and white stripes are constantly seen in pictures of Oriental life. From its size, usefulness, and value it came to represent clothing in general. It is made by taking two lengths of cloth, usually thick woollen stuff, each about seven feet long and two or two and a half feet wide. These are sewn together, and about a foot and a half is folded back at each end, making the piece about four feet

square. The doubled part is then over-edged along the
top, and an opening is made at each corner for the hand
to pass through. The cloak is sometimes made out of one
broad width, with no seam running across the back. Such,
most likely, was the garment without seam (John xix. 23).

When made as a light cloak for protection against dust
and heat, it is called a *burnous;* as worn by important
sheikhs, of black wool with needlework in colours on the
front and back, it is called a *mashlach;* in its commonest
form it is made of wool, goat-hair, or camel-hair, and
woven in broad alternate bands of black and white. This
is the *abaa* of the shepherd and peasant, the cloak worn by
night and day, and not to be kept as a pledge (Ex. xxii.
26). The peasants also have a somewhat smaller and
more convenient form of cloak woven in stripes of white
and red, and made of wool or cotton of the thickness of
sail-cloth. This is fitted with short sleeves, and is often
fastened with a girdle during active farm-work. The
cloak is referred to in Gen. xxv. 25; Josh. vii. 21; 2 Kings
ii. 14; Matt. iii. 4, v. 40.

(3) *Coat.*—This is worn over the shirt, resembling it in
length, but with the front cut open. Though still light,
it is of better material than the garment under it. The
overlapping fronts are clasped by the girdle, and form a
recess or pouch in which articles are carried with safety.
It resembles a clergyman's cassock or tightly-drawn dressing-gown, and is the most frequently seen dress in the
Oriental street. A man wearing this is clothed, but not
in the fullest sense *dressed.* It is all that is needed for
the house, the shop, and for working people moving about
in the town. The coat and cloak are contrasted in Matt.
v. 40; Luke vi. 29.

In Oriental dress this long tunic-coat is very commonly
divided at the girdle into two parts, the upper being a
short jacket or vest of richer and heavier material, often

highly ornamented after the manner of the priestly ephod, and the lower part is changed into skirt-trousers. For this a very wide sack is made with an opening at each corner through which the feet are passed, and it is gathered at the waist by a cord passing through the hem along the top. It is referred to in Ex. xxviii. 42, and Daniel iii. 21, *hosen* R.V.

ORIENTAL MALE COSTUMES.

(4) *Robe.*—In addition to the coat worn over the under dress there is another worn over the coat, like it in shape, except that it is ampler and worn loose without a belt or sash. It is, however, superior to the ordinary gown-coat in material, being generally of woollen cloth, and often lined with fur. It may be classed as a cloak, for in towns, among those who wear it, it is as much a public garment and completion of the costume as the large square cloak is in the country and villages. It is the professional dress of Government officials and religious dignitaries among the Moslems, and is worn by priests of the Oriental Church.

In Egypt it is generally a large black gown, not open
down the front, in shape like a surplice, and thus resembling the original under-dress of shepherd life. With
its opening for the head and neck protected by a cord, its
long folds and dignified appearance, it is suggestive of the
robe of the ephod worn by the high priest (Ex. xxviii.
31, 32). Joseph's "coat" (Gen. xxxvii. 3) may have been
the shepherd's under-dress adorned with embroidery, or it
may have been a robe to be worn over the gown, instead
of the ordinary broad cloak of the shepherds. For Bible
references see 1 Sam. ii. 19, xv. 27, xviii. 4, xxiv. 4;
Is. iii. 22; Zec. iii. 4; Luke xx. 46; Rev. vii. 13. Its
Arabic name means "a suit of exchange," and it is
always suggestive of public life, official dignity, and
special occasions.

(5) *Girdle* (1 Sam. xviii. 4; Ex. xxviii. 4; Is. iii. 24).—
The girdle is worn as a plain leather belt by Bedawîn and
the religious orders, and by the people of the villages and
towns in the form of a woven band like a saddle-girth, or
a large beautiful sash of striped silk. Money, bread, and
various small articles may be carried in the folds of the sash:
in the belt it is customary to have the material doubled
for a foot and a half from the buckle, thus forming a deep
and safe pocket. It is the girdle-pocket of Matt. x. 9.
The chief uses of the waist-band or girdle are to clasp the
gown and make a breast-pocket, to hold the drawn-up part
of the skirt in front, behind, or at the sides, when the
loins are girt for exercise; to make the purse just now
alluded to, and to hold the ink-horn of the writer.

(6) *Head-dress.*—This is translated bonnet, R.V. head-
tires in Ex. xxviii. 40, xxxix 28; turban, Dan. iii. 21, R.V.
marg. The sash and head-dress are the most ornamental
articles of Eastern dress. The latter is chiefly used as a
protection against the sun and a finish to the costume,
"for glory and beauty" (Ex. xxviii. 40; Is. lxi. 10).

To make it, a square yard of coloured cotton or silk with tassels is folded diagonally and arranged over the head and shoulders. It is held in position by several thick coils of soft woollen twist, or a smaller ornamental cord. The cloth thus worn on the head by Bedawîn and travellers generally is the napkin or handkerchief of Luke xix. 20; John xi. 44, xx. 7; Acts xix. 12. In villages this cloth is folded in a long strip, and wound round a small cotton or woollen cap to form a turban. Orientals do not remove

SHOES AND SANDALS.

the turban when entering a room; when for any purpose it is taken off it is laid down carefully and in as high a place as possible, as if in some way it represented their allegiance to their sovereign. The turban is carved in marble at the top of Moslem tombstones.

(7) *Sandals, shoes.*—These are associated with degradation (Ps. cviii. 9; Joshua v. 15; Luke ix. 5; John i. 27). In walking, Syrians from time to time pause to shake out the dust from their shoes, either by removing the shoe altogether, and slapping it on a stone or on the wall, or by letting it hang from the toe of the naked foot while the dust is shaken out. The original form consisted of a sole

with straps, by which it was tied to the foot, but a partial leather upper must soon have been found more convenient. The sandal is now seldom worn except by monks. Shepherds wear rough simple shoes, with leather gaiters covering the calf of the leg, on account of the rocks and thorns among which they climb. Shoes are seen in the Egyptian and Persian monuments.

SACRED FRINGE.

A very common kind of shoe is made of a piece of wood with a strap of leather over the instep. Those for brides are especially high and ornamental.

(8) *Border, fringe, skirt.*—Fringes made of the loose threads of the web are often seen at the end of Oriental cloth. It is the same with carpets, the threads being gathered and knotted into tassels. The most interesting survival is seen in the Jewish prayer-cloth, a covering of

white cotton or wool with black stripes for throwing over the head and figure during prayer, and called a tallith. It has small fringes along the sides, and a larger one at each corner inserted in a little square of coloured silk, and so arranged that its knots and threads, along with the numerical value of the Hebrew word for tassels, amount to 613, the number of commandments according to Rabbinical explanations. This tassel is put to the lips at certain times during the synagogue service to express obedience to the entire law (Mark vii. 6).

(9) *Female dress.*—The under-dress and gown-coat of women resembled those of men, and their upper robe corresponded to the suits of apparel or festival robes of men. These are referred to in 2 Sam. xiii. 18; Is. iii. 22, 23; Song of Sol. v. 3. There is still this resemblance in costume, the women's garments being, however, generally longer in proportion to the figure.

The turbans are made of deep bands of folded cloth, sometimes of ornamental silk, but usually of white cotton (Is. iii. 23). Until recently the head veil of the women of Mount Lebanon was drooped from a silver horn or upright funnel that was fixed securely on the head, and worn night and day. It was about a foot in height. The most characteristic features of female attire are the different veils. The women of the Moslem religion are very particular as to the screening of the face from view. Druze women expose one eye unveiled, and Christian and Jewish women merely veil the head and shoulders, but leave the face uncovered. The face veil is made of flowered gauze muslin (Is. iii. 19); there is also a larger and more ornamental lace veil for the head and shoulders. The *cauls* of Is. iii. 18 may refer to this latter class of veil. It is worn by women when making visits, and on their arrival it is the first duty of their entertainer to come forward and remove these veils as quickly as she can.

The same in its stronger original form is the head-dress of Bedawîn women. It is a shawl of stout, tough muslin wrapped round the head and neck and greater part of the figure (Is. iii. 22 ; Ruth iii. 15). The largest of all is the sheet-veil, called in Arabic *izar*, enveloping the whole body. The simplest form is a white sheet, but they are often made of rich, beautiful silk stuffs of native work-

FEMALE COSTUMES.

manship. A large square is folded in the middle and tied round the waist with a cord. The lower half thus forms a skirt, the upper being lifted over the shoulders and head to form a mantle-veil. Such are the *wimples* or shawls of Is. iii. 23. It is worn by Moslem women, and sometimes by others, when walking from place to place in the town.

(10) *Eye-paint*, consisting of a paste of brown antimony powder, is in common use. Applied to the eyes of children it is supposed to strengthen and protect them. When

used by women it is for the purpose of giving an enlarged
appearance and increased brilliancy to the eyes by means
of the gleaming black stain. It is kept in small ornamented vases having a rod attached to the stopper by
which the paint is applied to the eye-lashes. One of
Job's daughters was called Keren-happûch, horn of eye-
paint (Job xlii. 14). The practice is alluded to in
2 Kings ix. 30; Jer. iv. 30; Rev. iii. 18.

4. **The Family.**—In every land the home is the
nursery of all that is best and most beautiful in human
life. In Syria and Palestine there is no drink curse to
deaden and destroy natural feelings, and the parental
devotion of the poorest is as happy and self-denying as
that of the rich and refined. Nothing bewilders and
shocks the Oriental mind more than the paragraphs of
police news sometimes copied from English into Arabic
newspapers about the desertion and ill-treatment of children
by their parents. Occasionally an infant is laid by night
at the door of a convent or boarding-school, but almost
universally a child born into the poorest homes is welcomed
as a gift from God. Matters socially connected with the
family, such as neighbourhood, hospitality, and inheritance,
will be touched upon in the next chapter: we shall
here confine ourselves to the three chief events of family
life, namely, Birth, Marriage, and Death.

(1) *Birth.*—The leading and distinguishing feature of
Oriental family life is its preference of sons to daughters.
This of course is a result of social life rather than of domestic
affection. The want of public law and justice makes the
family a guild or union of common interests, not merely
for the cultivation of truth, obedience, and loving self-
sacrifice, but for marriage alliances, mercantile enterprises,
and social advancement generally. When a son marries,
he usually brings his young wife into the home of his
parents, to be for a time at least under his mother's

instruction. A daughter goes forth to be the purchased or bargained possession of another family, and gradually becomes identified with its interests. Her origin is not forgotten, however, and she is protected by her family influence. Often a wife who would be dismissed because of some petty provocation, is treated with respect and forbearance because any affront put upon her would alienate all her relatives. The union of all within the house under its recognised head against all that exists outside, is one of the leading ideas of Oriental life. An often quoted proverb says, "Better a thousand enemies outside the house than one inside." When an Oriental suspects that he is being over-reached, he can politely decline the proposal that seems injurious to his interests by saying, "Good-morning, neighbour, you are in your court and I am in mine." In Arabic the word *family* means "those who are cared for." Another proverb says, "In social matters act as kinsmen, in business matters be strangers." The moment the Oriental passes beyond his own door and the circle of his immediate neighbours, he encounters officials who have paid for their appointment, in whose election he has no vote, and over whose conduct he has no control. The home is not a training-place for noble service in the State, but a bulwark against its tyranny. Any family may grow into a clan the head of which may have sufficient means and influence to obtain a Government appointment, and then he can help and favour those who recognise his leadership. On account of this struggle for wealth and worldly promotion, and the importance of having an heir to succeed to it and use it, the birth of a male child brings joy to a family, and that of an infant daughter sorrow and disappointment (Jer. xx. 15 ; John xvi. 21). When a child is born, two or three local musicians are usually waiting outside to know if the new arrival be a boy or girl. If the former, they immediately beat the drum, and play upon whatever instruments they have, accompanying the din with improvised rhymes complimentary to the dignity of the family, and prophetic of the career lying before the son and heir. But the moment they learn from the silence and sad looks of the visitors that a daughter has been thrust upon the family, the drum is shouldered, and the musicians walk away. Music at such a time would be an unpaid affront. The grandmother sometimes refuses to visit a daughter who has thus brought discredit on the family. When natural affection and financial interest pull in opposite directions, victory too often goes to the latter. But God's ink does not lose colour although it is applied to such poor paper, and in spite of this disappointment at the beginning, the little daughter's claims to family love are soon more fully recognised.

This idea of the Oriental family as a business syndicate, quite as much as a sanctuary of affection, is expressed in the Koran, where it says, "Wealth and sons are the ornaments of life." Thus also in Psalm cxxvii. the family circle is compared to a quiver, and the sons are the arrows ready for service. Their father can command attention in the council of the elders at the city gate.

The new-born infant has its arms laid by its side and is wrapped in swaddling clothes. Among some of the peasantry the custom still prevails of rubbing the child's body with a powder of salt (Ezek. xvi. 4), but washing with water is usually avoided until after forty days. The little figure wrapped tightly in folds of cotton, and with its black eyes intensified by the eye-paint on the lashes, looks more like a mummy than a happy human child, and it is sometimes difficult to find the words of praise that the mother is expecting to hear.

The *names* of Oriental children, after the familiar Bible custom, usually express the parents' gratitude to God, or something connected with the personal appearance of the child or the circumstances under which it was born. Very frequently the name is given in remembrance of some relative. These names are thus personal registers of the happiness and hopes of their parents. Those of Jacob's family will be recalled as instances of this custom, and such names as Isaac, Ishmael, Moses, Ichabod, Samuel. It is not usual to call a son after his own father. The father's name is added as a kind of surname, as David, son-of-Jesse, Simon, son-of-Jonah. A name given after a member of the family in a former generation is a memorial of one who though still living is absent, and so might be forgotten. This seems to be the meaning of the question, "Why are they then baptized for the dead?" (1 Cor. xv. 29). To be named after some honoured relative implies a promise and hope that one child will inherit the character of the departed. According to this meaning, many of the ecclesiastical teachings connected with the rite in Christian baptism would float away with the other bubbles, and little would remain but the simple supreme purpose to live the very life of Christ.

A certain class of names is expressive of family anxiety and sorrow. Such are Dibb (bear), Nimr (leopard), and Saba (lion), given when one child after another has died in infancy, and it is hoped that the name of a common wild animal may take off the evil eye, and put a stop to such misfortune. This may have been the trouble when Caleb (dog) was born. Students of Oriental folk-lore find deeper meaning in such customs, but at the present day it is simply a form of humiliation to deliver a family from its dark fate, and in a dim superstitious way recognises the fact that a new life requires a new spirit.

The names of female children are usually taken from beautiful objects in nature, or pleasant graces of character.

Thus Astronomy gives Shems (sun), Kaukab and Nejmeh (star), Kumr (moon). Favourite flower-names are Zambak (lily), Yasmîn (jessamine), and Wurdeh (rose). Jewellery is of course very popular : the school register is always richly ornamented with such names as Lulu (pearl), Almaz (diamond), Zumurrud (emerald). Many again are suggestive of the pleasant appearance or kindly dispositions of their owners. Such are Selma (peace), Simha (joy), Farideh (special), Latîfeh (gracious), Sultaneh (princess), Jamîleh (pleasant).

Bible examples are Jemima (dove), Tabitha or Dorcas (gazelle), Rhoda (rose), Rachel (lamb), Salome (peace), Deborah (bee), Esther (star).

A quaintly sad name is Kafah (enough), an implied remonstrance, meaning that after the birth of several daughters the parents would have reverently preferred to have had at least one son.

In the East there is very little of the child-life with which we are familiar in our Western homes. Great allowance is made for the impulsive ways of children, but parents never attempt to draw them into companionship, and there is no literature for young people. Thus in the *Arabian Nights* the interval between birth and marriage is usually a blank. Dolls are greatly enjoyed by the little girls, but Moslems, Jews, and Druzes find a taint of idolatry in them. Boys play with marbles, tops, and balls, and both boys and girls imitate in their games the things that occupy the serious attention of their elders. Thus juvenile bands form into a marriage procession with sword-play, music, and shouting. They dramatise funerals and make lamentation in the same way. Bedawîn robbers attacking travellers and law courts are also popular. The selling of Joseph, the sorrows of Job, and the raising of Lazarus are described in poetry, which is learnt by many, and passes down unchanged from generation to generation like our nursery rhymes. The account of Job's misfortunes, for example, tells how his wife cut her hair and her husband's to sell it for food, and such graphic touches come to be regarded as part of the original story. It is easy to conceive how a scribe copying one of the books of Scripture might introduce an explanatory comment from such floating traditions. The references to the book of Jashar are perhaps instances of this (Josh. x. 13; 2 Sam. i. 18). The children in Christ's time evidently played at marriage and funeral processions as they do at the present time. The lack of response to His appeal and the impossibility of His complying with Jewish expectations could be compared to children playing in the open market-place, until, wearied with their sport or distracted by other things, they paid no attention either to the marriage music or funeral wail (Matt. xi. 17). Among the little girls of the East the chief entertainment is to play at bride. One of their number is selected and dressed up with contributions from the others, and sits with downcast eyes and folded hands to be admired by her young companions.

2. The chief event in Oriental family life is *Marriage*. This is usually planned by parents in the infancy of their children. The formal betrothal may take place some years before the marriage. The bridegroom-elect sends a present to the girl, the dowry is settled, and if sometime afterwards the engagement be broken off, the young woman, if a Jewess, cannot be married to any one else without receiving first a paper of divorce from the rabbi.

The marriage is a great occasion of festivity, sometimes prolonged over several days. To be omitted in the invitations is a grave offence. A proverb says: "He who does not invite me to his marriage will not have me at his funeral."

The wedding customs of to-day strongly resemble those mentioned in Scripture, but do not exactly repeat them.

The Jews introduce European elements, the Christians have new traditions belonging to the Christian Church, and the Moslems who usually preserve most of the ancient practices are here affected by the severe seclusion of women.

At a Jewish wedding the most interesting feature is the canopy under which the bridegroom and bride sit or stand during the ceremony. It is erected in the court or large room of the house where the guests are assembled, and is made of palm-branches and embroidered cloth. It is suggestive of the dome sometimes seen above pulpits, and gives to the wedding the appearance of a coronation. In Is. lxi. 10 the bridegroom is described, R.V. marg., as decked like a priest, and he still wears at such a time the prayer-cloak of public worship called the tallith. The Jews say "the bridegroom is a king." The husband is priest and king in his own household. Amid all the countries in which the Jews are scattered, and the different languages that they learn to speak, the canopy is called by its Hebrew name, the Huppah. The sight of the robed bridegroom issuing from the canopy (tabernacle) and receiving with smiles the congratulations of his friends suggested the simile of the sunrise in Ps. xix. 6. At a Jewish marriage one item of sad significance is never omitted. The glass that holds the wine of marriage consecration is dropped on the floor and broken to pieces. This is explained as a memorial of the destroyed temple, and teaches the Jew that in the moment of his own supreme happiness he must not forget the deep sorrows of his nation. The thought recalls Ps. cxxxvii. 6.

In the Parable of the Ten Virgins (Matt. xxv. 1-13), the reader of Scripture naturally wishes to know where the maidens were when they slumbered and slept, and where and why the bridegroom tarried.

The following description will throw some light on those difficulties :—Oriental marriages usually take place in the evening. Among Jews and Christians the ceremony is usually performed in the house of the bride's parents, though among the Christians frequently in the church; among the Moslems always in the house of the bridegroom. The whole attention is turned to the public arrival of the bridegroom to receive the bride prepared for him and waiting in the house among her female attendants.

If we make allowance for some changes in detail caused by their rules as to the seclusion of women, the Moslem customs are those which help us most in trying to understand how marriages took place in Bible times. During the day the bride is conducted to the house of her future husband, and she is there assisted by her attendants in putting on the marriage robes and jewellery. During the evening, the women who have been invited congregate in the room where the bride sits in silence, and spend the time commenting on her appearance, complimenting the relatives, discussing various family matters, and partaking of sweetmeats and similar refreshments.

As the hours drag on their topics of conversation become exhausted, and some of them grow tired and fall asleep. There is nothing more to be done, and everything is in readiness for the reception of the bridegroom, when the cry is heard outside announcing his approach.

The bridegroom meanwhile is absent spending the day at the house of one of his relatives. There, soon after sunset, that is between seven and eight o'clock, his male friends begin to assemble. Their work for the day is over; they have taken a hasty supper, and dressed themselves, and have come to spend the evening with the bridegroom and then escort him home. The time is occupied with light refreshments, general conversation and the recitation of poetry in praise of the two families chiefly concerned and of the bridegroom in particular. After all have been courteously welcomed and their congratulations received, the bridegroom, about eleven o'clock, intimates his wish to set out. Flaming torches are then held aloft by special bearers, lit candles are handed at the door to each visitor as he goes out, and the procession sweeps slowly along towards the house where the bride and her female attendants are waiting. A great crowd has meanwhile assembled on the balconies, garden-walls, and flat roofs of the houses on each side of the road. It is always an impressive spectacle to watch the passage of such a brilliant retinue under the starry stillness of an Oriental night. The illumination of the torches and candles not only makes the procession itself a long winding array of moving lights, but throws into sharp relief the white dresses and thronging faces of the spectators seen against the sombre walls and dark sky. The bridegroom is the centre of interest. Voices are heard whispering, "There he is! there he is!" From time to time women raise their voices in the peculiar shrill, wavering shriek by which joy is expressed at marriages and other times of family and public rejoicing. The sound is heard at a great distance, and is repeated by other voices in advance of the procession, and thus intimation is given of the approach half an hour or more before the marriage escort arrives. It was during this interval that the foolish virgins hurried out in quest of oil for their lamps. Along the route the throng becomes more dense, and begins to move with the retinue bearing the lights. As the house is approached the excitement increases, the bridegroom's pace is quickened, and the alarm is raised in louder tones and more repeatedly, "*He is coming, he is coming!*"

Before he arrives, the maidens in waiting come forth with lamps and candles a short distance to light up the entrance, and do honour to the bridegroom and the group of relatives and intimate friends around him. These pass into the final rejoicing and the marriage supper; the others

who have discharged their duty in accompanying him to
the door, immediately disperse, and the door is shut.

Such is the simple incident in the earthly home that
has found such wonderful correspondences in the heavenly
life.   The bridal procession has been taken into the house
of Parable, and there robed with beautiful vesture of
spiritual truth.   If we are careful to interpret the latter
by the former, we shall learn : (1) from the bride's
adorning what varied and skilful attendance the Church,
the Bride of Christ, needs, in order to wear properly
the Bridegroom's gifts ; (2) from the bright, forward-
moving procession, that every servant of Christ should be a
light-bearer and never stand still ; and (3) from the turning
of all eyes upon the bridegroom, how great is the trespass
when any Church official or creed-banner displaces or obscures
the great central personality, the Lord Jesus Christ.

3. *Funerals.*—When a death occurs in an Oriental
home, a wail is immediately raised that announces the
sad event to those living in the neighbourhood.   It is
customary and expected at such times of sorrow that the
relatives should tear their hair and clothes, beat the
breast, weep and cry aloud until sheer physical exhaustion
brings on a necessary reaction of dulness and depression.
Orientals are unsurpassed in the quiet, unmurmuring
acceptance of the will of God ; but, in giving social proof
and manifestation of their felt loss, the expression of
grief becomes the chief burden of grief.   The wail at the
moment of death, and the lamentation around the corpse
during the short interval before interment, are referred to
in Gen. xii. 30 ; Mark v. 38 ; John xi. 31 ; and Acts ix. 39.
The tears of Christ at the grave of Lazarus have been
a comfort in many a darkened home, allowing the heart
to feel and tell its bitterness, even while faith in God
remains sure and strong.   Some of the common language
of Oriental lamentation is preserved in Jer. xxii. 18.

Weeping relatives lean over the cold form of him who was so recently interested in the smallest affairs of the family and the chief object of its ministry, and with words of loving endearment they plead for a response from the lips that never move and the face that makes no sign. Other names, the names of those in the family who have died lately, are mentioned and make the tears gush forth afresh. The women who attend professionally to assist at such lamentation are skilful in interweaving family references and in improvising poetry in praise of the departed. When a new band of mourners arrives from a neighbouring village, they lift up their arms and exclaim, "Hope is cut off!" (Job viii. 13; Is. lvii. 10; Ezek. xxxvii. 11). When a young person dies unmarried, the funeral lamentation is made more pathetic by first going through some of the forms of a wedding ceremony. That which is is thus contrasted with what might have been. Thus Jephthah's daughter bewailed her virginity in the presence of the fate that awaited her (Judges xi. 37).

In the warm climate of the East the interval between death and interment has to be very brief, the funeral generally taking place the same day, or on the day following. The formulated frenzy that to some extent displaces true grief in the house of mourning often turns into pious selfishness on the way to the grave. Among modern Orientals, accompanying a funeral procession is called *attending the merit*, an act that will secure a reward from God.

Thus when the letter of useful form is killed by slavish obedience, religious hypocrisy, its next of kin, comes as the avenger of blood and takes away the last remnants of natural feeling.

Among the Jews a cemetery is solemnly called the House of Eternity (Eccl. xii. 5), and sometimes the House of the Living.

CHAPTER VI

SOCIAL, POLITICAL, AND RELIGIOUS LIFE

Escape from self is better than escape from a lion.
There are two that are never satisfied—the seeker of knowledge
   and the seeker of wealth.
The best wealth is that which is pleasing to God.

Syrian Proverbs.

THE present chapter brings us to a point of view that
commands a very extensive and variegated prospect.
It is the illustration of Scripture from the social life,
public government, and literary, scientific, and religious
institutions of the East.

1. Oriental Villages.—(1) *Their origin.*—The landscape of the East shows no farm-houses scattered here and
there over the plains and valleys.   Those who cultivate the
soil in any district build their houses beside each other in a
village.   As already mentioned, one of the chief reasons
for this was the unsettled state of the country.   The
produce and various possessions of the farmers, and their
own lives also, had to be protected against the shepherd
tribes.   Further, the leading sheikhs of the different clans
were constantly at war with each other, and the peasantry
who tilled the property of their local prince had to make
common cause with him.   His enemies were their enemies.
How thorough this submission must have been may be
inferred from the recent remark of an old sheikh, who

maintained that government on the present national plan was not so good as that of the old system of ruling families. When asked what he meant by good government, he pointed to a large gray rock and said : "When I said to one of my people, 'That stone is red,' he used to answer 'It is red'; if I said 'No, it is green,' he would answer 'It is green.' That is good government, but it is lost now."

These local feuds meant a constant exposure to attack, and the village became offensively and defensively the home of the clan, as the house was of the family.

A third reason pointing in the same direction was the necessity of water. This was required not only for the inhabitants and their animals, but also for vegetable gardens. In this way the village often got its name from the fountain (*'ain*) or well (*beer*) beside which it was built, coupled with the cliff, tree, meadow, castle, or some such natural feature in the vicinity. Bible examples of this were Abel-ma-im, Beersheba, Endor.

(2) *Appearance.*—The small villages of the peasantry in the wheat plains are mere mud-brick hovels, allotted by the proprietor to those who till the surrounding fields. Those on the hill-sides are built of limestone; their inhabitants have more independence and greater variety of occupation, and the whole appearance of such villages is very much better. The houses with their flat roofs look like so many large boxes that have rolled down from above and been suddenly arrested in their descent. They are often so near each other that the door of one leads out to the flat roof of the house below it. The white walls gleam out of the surrounding mulberry foliage, the monotony being usually broken by the larger dimensions and better architecture of the sheikh's house, and sometimes the houses cluster round the prominent nucleus of the village church, leaving a few to straggle up the slope

towards the ridge where the old shrine-tomb under its
oak-tree gives a picturesque outline to the background.

(3) *Village life.*—The farmers go out to their work in
the fields, which are often at a considerable distance, and
usually they do not return till sunset. This is the *going
forth* referred to in the Bible in connection with the labours
of the field (Ps. civ. 23, cxxvi. 6 ; Luke xiv. 19, xv. 25). It
is village life that is also referred to in Isaiah i. 3, where
it is said, "The ox knoweth his owner, and the ass his
master's crib." At sunset, the village cattle and donkeys
that have been out all day in the neighbouring common and
bare fields are brought by the herdsman to the entrance of
the village. There they all leave him, and find their way
through the village lanes each to its own place of rest for
the night. Some of the trades that receive their fullest
development in the towns have their beginning among
the peasantry of the village. The village oven is heated
on alternate days ; one of the inhabitants does simple
carpenter work ; another shoes the horses, mules, and
donkeys, and is resorted to when branding is considered
necessary ; once, or oftener, according to the size of the
village, the butcher has mutton or kid's-flesh for sale,
and the muleteer transports merchandise between the
village and the neighbouring towns. Life is very simple,
kindly, and laborious ; there is intimate knowledge of each
other's affairs, and ready sympathy in all times of family
rejoicing and sorrow. The arrival of any stranger is immediately known through the village, and any of its residents
returning from a journey is courteously waited upon and
welcomed (Ruth i. 19). The women have much to speak
about at the fountain as they wait their turn to fill the
jar, and the elders meet in the evening to discuss village
matters and receive and give the latest news. Feuds
abound between the rival sects, the older and the more
recent residents, and the families that compete for the

place of chief influence and honour. All, however, unite in resenting any affront put upon the village by those who do not belong to it.

The annual capitation tax, or sum paid by each adult to the Government, is reckoned and paid in the village in which he is born. His relatives are there, and any ancestral land he may have inherited. If he goes elsewhere he must first appoint those who shall be responsible for the payment. Though his employment may make him live in another village, and his children and grandchildren may have been born and brought up away from the original home, their tax also must be paid there. Thus Joseph returned to Bethlehem because he was of the lineage of David (Luke ii. 4).

2. The City.—The growth of the town or city is chiefly due to the neighbourhood of large wheat-growing plains, or of extensive vineyards, or to its appointment as a seat of government, or the opportunity of maritime commerce. In ancient times the halting-places on the great caravan-routes became towns of wealth and luxury.

(1) *The wall.*—The great high wall enclosing all the houses continued and emphasised the chief purpose of the house and the village, namely, protection. The distant glimmer of the white turreted wall rising out of the bare desert or green surrounding foliage was a vision of comfort and encouragement to the weary traveller. Once within these walls there would be rest and release from danger, the society of those he loved, and the supply of every want. These features of the ancient city appear in the description of the New Jerusalem (Rev. xxi.), and give their beautiful symbolism to the mediæval hymns and meditations about "the city of God."

Under the more settled conditions of the present day in Syria and Palestine the city walls are being rapidly obscured by the houses of the open suburbs.

As the ancient masons had no explosives for blasting purposes, the stones were laboriously cut out of the solid rock. As it was less trouble to cut one thick one than two thinner ones, some of these stones are of gigantic size. Those of the wall of Jerusalem are very large, and

CITY GATE.

in their variety of Jewish, Roman, Crusading, and Saracen styles of workmanship they are emblematic of the different nations that have received the Gospel.

(2) *The gate.*—The city gate is often referred to in Scripture. It is large and massive, made of oak with a facing of studded iron or bronze. A foot or two above the ground there is inserted in the middle of the great door a smaller one about $2\frac{1}{2} \times 2$ feet in size, by which the

porter at his discretion may admit one who arrives after
sunset. The city gate was a precaution against the
approach of an unseen enemy attacking the city under
cover of the night. Hence the Heavenly city, where
there is no darkness and nothing hostile can ever enter,
has its gates always open in token of friendly welcome
(Rev. xxi. 25).

(3) *The streets.*—The Oriental street is a mere lane
for foot passengers and baggage animals. No names are
needed for the chief streets, as each is set apart for a
particular trade or the sale of special commodities. You
have only to enter it to know when you are in Vegetable
Street, Perfumers' Street, Silversmiths' Street, etc. The
narrowness of the streets shelters the tradesmen and
passers-by from the heat of the sun. Here and there a
high roof is thrown over the street, deepening the shade
and protecting against rain. These intervals of subdued
light make the dazzle all the greater when a widening or
turn of the street allows the sunlight to pour down upon
the variegated costumes and bright wares of an Oriental
town. A walk through the bazaars of Damascus with its
silk stuffs, cloth of gold, ornaments of brass, and ancient
perfumes of incense and various gums, makes it easy to
follow and realise the prophet's description of ancient
Tyre (Ezek. xxvii.)

As one leaves the bazaars or rows of shops, and walks
through the quiet part of the town occupied by dwelling-
houses, one is impressed by the suspicious, prohibitive
appearance of the houses. No windows look out upon the
streets near the ground, and those of the upper rooms are
closely latticed. No one is seen, and no sound is heard,
unless occasionally the shrill, peevish voices of women
engaged in some domestic quarrel. Beautiful houses, with
large marble courts adorned with fountains and evergreen
trees, and having reception-rooms enriched with carpets and

ornamental carvings, are entered by a narrow lane and a
mere stable door.   It is more easily defended in any time
of sudden attack, and its humble appearance averts the
punishment of pride and the curse of the evil eye.   The
street is for the passer-by, and the house is a sacred and
guarded enclosure.   Everything within it speaks of
welcome, and everything without of exclusion.   In cities
where there are Jews, Christians, and Moslems, these
occupy separate quarters, forming a city within the city,
with the religious name for a bond of union.

No description of an Oriental city would be complete
without some reference to the dogs that lie about in the
streets.   They are of wolf-like appearance, black or tawny-
yellow in colour, lazy and unclean, and tolerated because
they devour the kitchen refuse that is thrown into the
street, and act as sanitary police without payment.   The
town is carefully divided by them into districts, each of
which is occupied by the dogs belonging to it, and beyond
which they must never pass.   When one of their number
goes beyond his proper boundary, the dog who first sees
him gives a yelp of alarm ; this is caught up and passed
on by those who hear it, and in a minute or two the whole
pack is seen tearing along like a fire-brigade towards the
point where the first bark was heard.   If the intruder has
not already made his escape, he is rolled over, worried,
and pursued a good way into his own district.

Lying in the road, a menace and impediment to ordinary
traffic, most numerous where men most congregate, and yet
seeking no real companionship with them, happiest when
twenty of them can get together and jump upon one poor
offender, and disturbing the public peace with their code
of honour about dust-heaps and old refuse—such are the
similarities that unite Oriental dogs and Pharisees (Phil.
ii. 2).

3. **Neighbourhood.**—As Oriental houses are always

either in villages or towns, the fact of neighbourhood is of great social importance. All the Bible references to friends, neighbours, and sojourners apply to these relationships at the present day.

The Oriental is never alone, and the most numerous and familiar class of proverbs is that which deals with the necessity of neighbourhood, and all the advantages and disadvantages connected with it.

Its influence for good or evil is described in the maxims : " If you live forty days with people, you will then either leave them or become like them " ; " We are your neighbours, and have learnt from you." To one about to build or rent a house, or go on a journey, the advice is given : " Consider the neighbour before the house, and the companion before the road."

Identification of interest is taught in the words : " If it is well with your neighbour, it is well with you ; " " He who cropped your neighbour will crop you ; " and " A loaf more or less, but never let your neighbour want."

The patience due to this relationship is stated in the proverb : " Your neighbour is your neighbour though he should act otherwise." The thought of Prov. xxv. 17 is repeated in figurative form : " If your friend be honey do not eat him." Prov. xxvii. 10 is constantly quoted.

The neighbours are present on all occasions of family sorrow and joy (Luke xv. 6, 9). Such intimate knowledge of each other is implied in the words, " I have called you friends " (John xv. 15). The commandment against bearing false witness is framed for the special protection of the neighbour, as, in his constant contact with those around him, he may at times give offence and so provoke reprisals. The strength of the Oriental law of neighbourhood is seen in the various abuses it endures. Its kindly provisions originated under circumstances of social equality, mutual helpfulness, and common danger, but the law of neighbourly duty as an obligation of honour is often appealed to by those who have no opportunity or thought of doing anything in return. Thus the merchant is expected to sell cheaper and the doctor to lower his fees to those in the neighbourhood, though they may have no acquaintance with them, and even the European manager of a Waterworks Company will be urged to reduce the rate for those who live near his dwelling-house. Oriental neighbourhood enlarges the family, but contracts the world. It is a trade union on family lines. Any one outside of the circle is a foreigner, alien, enemy, heathen (2 Kings v. 20). Christ recognised the law of neighbourhood in commanding that the preaching of the Gospel should begin at Jerusalem, the place where the Apostles were, but its terminus was the ends of the earth. The parable of the Good Samaritan taught the true meaning and fulfilment of neighbourhood. In the Sermon on the Mount it was pointed out that a religion of mere social selfishness and mutual catering was impossible for those who would be children of the Highest (Matt. v. 43-48).

4. **Hospitality.**—The East is celebrated for its laws of hospitality. Among the Bedawîn and those living in remote villages these laws retain their primitive meaning and veneration, and in the towns the parade of compliment with which a caller or guest is received is still suggestive of the original custom. Taken in connection with the laws of neighbourhood and the generally avaricious tone of Oriental life, the importance assigned to hospitality is not only beautiful but mysterious. The attentions shown to invited guests (Luke xiv. 12) present no difficulty, as they belong rather to the courtesies of neighbourhood; also the motive of the feast of Ahasuerus is always more or less in evidence (Est. i. 4).

The peculiar feature of Oriental hospitality is that it commands the most devoted service to be rendered to those

who are passing strangers, and have none of the claims
that belong to kinship and acquaintance. Towards an
explanation of the mystery two facts deserve to be
mentioned.

(1) There is *the greatness of the favour.*—It is an appeal
to what is noblest and best in the human heart. The
stranger who comes to the door has reached his limit.
He can go no farther (Rev. iii. 20). He is at the mercy
of those within, either to receive him or rob him. The
moment he enters by permission he becomes virtually the
master of the house. He is told that the house is his.
The owner waits upon him, all the supplies of the house
are for his necessities, all its strength is for his defence.
The guest's act of trust is responded to by a chivalrous
readiness on the part of the host to lay down his life for
the stranger.

In addition to the fact of safety, there is the great
comfort of rest after labour, food and drink after exhaustion,
and society after solitude. A proverb says, "He who sows
kindness reaps gratitude," and the many worries and un-
expected dilemmas incident to Oriental travel make the
moment of release from them one of heart-felt thankfulness.

(2) *The sanctity of the guests.*—These customs were
established long before travel was undertaken in the
interests of commerce or exploration, and some very strong
reason was needed to make a man face the dangers and
hardships of a journey. The arrival of a stranger was a
rare occurrence, and the law of hospitality forbade any
inquiry as to where he had come from or where he was
going, until the expiry of at least three days showed that
his case was not one of urgency or personal danger. It
would be generally supposed that the reason of his journey
was either flight from an enemy, some grave family
necessity, or the performance of a religious vow. With
regard to the first of the three causes, the bitterness of the

blood-feuds made every entertainer feel that he might be the next to need shelter. The arrival of the stranger showed that whatever his trouble might be, God had so far favoured him, and a grave danger was thus incurred by any one who treated him with unkindness. Hence a mysterious sacredness became connected with a guest, and with the duty of protecting him and ministering to his wants. There was a deeper necessity than that of hunger and thirst ; "*I was a stranger and ye took me in*" (Matt. xxv. 35). The Koran echoes the exhortation of Heb. xiii. 2 by the negative statement, " The house that receives no guests never receives angels."

The act by which the claim of hospitality is established is the partaking of the family bread, salt or water, or even the laying hold upon the tent pole. If a fugitive approaches a shepherd in the wilderness he will be invited to partake of the bread and cheese which the latter has in his scrip, and the moment he has done so the shepherd must protect him against any pursuers who may arrive to kill him. The appointment of the Cities of Refuge in the land of Israel will occur to the mind in this connection as an endeavour to mitigate the ferocities of the blood-feuds by national legislation.

A case occurred some years ago near Tripoli in Syria, which shows what a strong sense of duty and honour is pledged for the protection of a guest. A man had committed manslaughter, and in his flight from the avengers of blood came to the mountain hut of a shepherd. The shepherd was absent with his flock, and the fugitive begged and received protection in the name of God from his wife and young son. Half an hour afterwards the house was surrounded by horsemen. Their law of courtesy made it impossible for them to enter the only room of the house, which was sacred as being the women's apartment, and they demanded that the criminal should be brought forth.

The poor woman came to the door holding by the hand her son, twelve years of age, and said, " I cannot surrender my guest, but take my only son and kill him instead." Her resolute chivalry so impressed them that after a short pause they told her that for her sake the fugitive was pardoned and free.   Then they rode away.

This devotion has no thought of the sanctity of life for its own sake, or the claims of humanity as such.   The guest-law is entirely a creation of place and circumstance. When a traveller is met by Bedawîn in the desert, their ordinary salutation is "Strip!"   If resistance is offered they think very lightly of the crime of murder.   The authority of the guest-law within its own area shows to what a deep state of misery the Israelites and their friends must have been reduced when Jael killed her guest, and such profanation of the law of hospitality was publicly commended.

In the East work of any kind is generally regarded as degrading, but there are three recognised exceptions, namely, a man's service to his guest, to his household, and to his horse.

5. **Property.**—(1) *Possession.*—Land in the East is held in three ways.

(*a*) The arable ground around a village, like the pasture land, is held in common by its inhabitants, and allotted in proportion to the number of oxen belonging to a villager for the purpose of ploughing.   The first disciples at Jerusalem applied this already familiar principle to their personal wealth (Acts ii. 44, 45).

(*b*) Under more settled government the above arrangement presented difficulties in the collection of taxes and the punishment of those who failed to pay them.   Thus land came into the possession of personal owners, or was bought in the name of a commercial company.

(*c*) Large portions of the country belong to the Govern-

ment, as crown lands. These are rented to the highest
bidder, who re-lets them to peasant cultivators at such a
price as will secure him a profit by the transaction.

(2) *Cultivation.* — The peasants who till the land
belonging to a large proprietor have houses built for them,
and as they generally remain in charge even when the
land changes owners they thus become in a manner serfs
upon it.

In grain-land, if the owner supplies seed and oxen for
ploughing, and pays the government-tithe, the peasant-
labourer in charge gets one-fourth of the produce; if the
owner only pays the tax the peasant has two-thirds, or
one-half if the land be very remunerative in proportion to
the labour expended upon it.

For vineyards and the cultivation of fruit-trees generally,
the peasant receives for his labour one-third of the produce,
but after some years, during which the property has been
improved by cultivation and additional vines and trees, he
is entitled to one-half, and can claim to be regarded as co-
proprietor (Matt. xxi. 33-41).

(3) *Sale.* — When property, either in the form of house
and garden or cultivated land, is to be sold, the particulars
are mentioned with elaborate detail, and the deed of sale
is attested in the local court and recorded in its books.
These formalities, however, often afford very insecure protection to the purchaser. After the money has been paid
other part-owners present their claims and prohibit the new
owner from taking possession.

When land is sold, the first right of purchase belongs
to a partner, and after him to a neighbour, especially if
the same water irrigates both lands.

When it is desired to defeat his claim, and also to
obviate the danger of future claimants appearing to
dispute the ownership, a peculiar device is resorted to.

The land is divided into two sections, A and B.

Thus a piece of ground, 400 yards square, is to be sold for £300.   Section A is about one-sixth of the whole— a mere strip adjoining that of the objectionable neighbour, and its price is fixed at £200 : the remaining five-sixths of the ground are priced at £100.   The two sections are bought on these terms by the new purchaser, and he and the seller repair together to the court to have it made legal.   Here the neighbour may enter his protest and obtain the strip A nearest his own, but he must pay £200 for it.   He has no claim on B, because the new owner has now a neighbour's claim on it, from having paid the price of A.   If the original neighbour should purchase the strip A for £200, he could only sell it to him who purchased the B section because the latter has now the pre-emption right of a neighbour!

Much of the artificiality that pervades the Jewish observance of the law is doubtless due to the Talmudic incorporation of strictly religious duties with petty legal details about property.   They are thus reduced to the same moral level, and the business instinct that seeks its own advantage, and purchases in the cheapest market, is put on the alert to find out the minimum of service that will secure a name for piety and a place in the heavenly inheritance.   The purchase of property among modern Orientals often resembles Abraham's transaction with the sons of Heth (Gen. xxiii.)   It is usually a matter abounding in indirect preliminaries, solemn conference, ostentatious politeness, shameless lying, and hard haggle.

(4) *Inheritance.*—In modern Oriental law property is divided equally among the sons, each daughter receiving half the share of a son.

6. Law and Government.—The administration of law reveals the best and worst of Oriental life.   The basing of statutes on moral and religious principles was originally intended to teach forbearance and charity by bringing

litigants before the Unseen Judge of all. It had much in
its favour as long as those principles were honestly
interpreted and reverently obeyed, but when they ceased
to be regarded, and public opinion was intimidated and
debased, the judge could do very much as he pleased.   It
became of the first importance to secure the personal
favour of the judge.   The unjust judge of the parable
(Luke xviii. 1-7), who had no fear of God, would find it very
easy to disregard men.   An Arabic proverb says, "When
the judge's mule dies, everybody goes to the funeral ;
when the judge himself dies, nobody goes."

Bribery and perjury are the two sides of the cloven
hoof in both ancient and modern courts of law in the East.

Thus Samuel, in reviewing his administration, emphasised
the fact that he had never taken bribes, and the corruption
of the judges in the kingdom of Israel is stigmatised by the
prophets as one of the chief causes of the nation's rejection
and ruin.

Modern Orientals are extremely subtle and insidious in
their manner of making presents.   The fact that "a man's
gift maketh room for him" (Prov. xviii. 16) is constantly
acted upon.   In private life, the sending of a gift is usually a
prelude to a request for some favour or exercise of influence.
In Oriental courtesy the rejection of a gift is a serious
affront, and its acceptance implies a debt of honour calling for some suitable return.   Sometimes the authorities
plainly indicate that money is required, but usually the
initiative comes from the people.   Upright pashas and
judges for a time purge the administration of these abuses,
but when they are removed the contending parties who
seek the favour of their successors soon restore the old
corruptions.   Religious influence, instead of helping the
cause of mercy and justice, runs in the line of ecclesiastical
parties and institutions, and these always do battle for
their own ends.   At every point the religious sanction

makes a family covenant, and the family bond in Oriental use and wont protects its membership without regard to the rights of common citizenship or the supreme claims of truth.

Perjury is very common. In the New Testament one is shocked to read how the Pharisees, the leaders of religion, got witnesses to swear to what they either knew nothing about or knew to be untrue. Such witnesses are only too easily obtained for any emergency in the East, and in this respect the witness of priests and monks is proverbially untrustworthy.

Prisons. — The Oriental prisons of the present day vividly recall the allusions to those of ancient times.

There is the common prison for debt, arrears of taxes, and ordinary offences. Besides this there is the inner or underground prison for criminals, called the prison of blood. There Paul and Silas were kept (Acts xvi. 24), and though cut off from companionship with others, their voices were heard as "they sang praises unto God."

The difficulty of getting out of prison (Matt. v. 26) is exemplified not only in the postponement of the day of trial, but after the term of imprisonment has expired, in meeting the various claims of the jailors, such as a fee exacted for the handcuffs or chain utilised by the prisoner. Most of these abuses resemble those in the English prisons at the beginning of the eighteenth century.

Owing to this hard treatment and the frequent miscarriage of justice, and also the kindly uncritical sympathies of Orientals generally, imprisonment is regarded as a misfortune rather than a disgrace. Friends go about to collect money for the relief or release of those imprisoned. The Saviour did not mean that humanity should cease from hoping, serving, and rescuing at the prison gates (Matt. xxv. 36).

7. Rich and Poor.—(1) *Poverty.*—Beggars are very

numerous in the East. The usual types are given in Luke xiv. 13, "the poor, the maimed, the lame, and the blind." Besides these there are those who are simply indolent. An Arabic proverb says, "Begging is an easy trade, only the standing at the door is tiresome."

Among those who suffer from bodily infirmity, loss of limb by machinery is seldom met with, but disease in skin, blood, and bone is frequent and often assumes loathsome forms, the chief instance being that of leprosy.

The commonest and most pathetic form of infirmity that has nothing repulsive about it is blindness. Some of these blind beggars, either led by children or guiding themselves by their long sticks, move about from door to door, but usually they are found at regular places in the town. The blind and lame are conducted or carried to the doors of churches at the time of service, especially on fast days, and line the steps at marriage and funeral ceremonies. They also congregate in front of chief houses on any occasion of family rejoicing or sorrow.

Sometimes blindness, deformity, and disease meet in one poor shrivelled frame; and year after year the beggar is borne daily to his place at a public corner in the town, or at the end of a bridge on its outskirts, and sitting on the ground under the rain or burning sun, with the dust flying over him in clouds from carriages and baggage animals, he recites the promises of God to those who care for the poor. Thus it was with Lazarus at the rich man's gate (Luke xvi. 20), Bartimæus by the road-side at Jericho (Mark x. 46), and the cripple at the Temple gate (Acts iii. 2).

(2) *Mode of appeal.*—This is sometimes a simple statement of poverty, "I am poor," "I want a loaf of bread," "Give me the price of a loaf" (half-penny).

The plea is occasionally enforced by the expressive gesture of bringing the forefinger across the teeth and holding it up as a proof that there is absolutely no trace of food there. It is "cleanness of teeth" (Am. iv. 6).

Usually, however, the appeal is to religious feeling or duty.

As the beggar stands at the door, he calls out, "I am your guest! I am God's guest! God will direct you! God will recompense you! God will preserve your children! God will prolong your days!" If this fails, he tries the effect of rebuke : "Is there nothing here for God?" "You are all servants!" When there is nothing for him, he is told, "God will give you! The Lord will relieve you!" (James ii. 16).

The beggars are thus the great street-preachers of the East. The thought of 1 Sam. ii. 7 pervades the whole relationship of poverty and wealth. God has a purpose in giving wealth and permitting poverty (Prov. xiv. 31).

Beggars apportion the shops among them, and at the close of the week go their rounds to get their allowance. The rich and poor are thus brought into personal touch with each other, but Oriental benevolence has no thought of attacking the cause of poverty (Deut. xv. 11). The absence of alcohol prevents the Oriental beggar from having the degraded appearance of the Western tramp, and the cause of poverty, apart from cases of pure indolence, is usually found in sickness, or the loss of the breadwinner in the family or his indefinite imprisonment. A proverb says, "Never teach an orphan how to weep."

A great deal of Oriental almsgiving arises from the love of praise, or a superstitious hope that coppers given away may atone for pounds obtained by cheating. Almsgiving has a high place among the religious virtues of the East (Deut. xv. 10 ; Prov. xxviii. 27). In the Jewish synagogue there is often a box for receiving anonymous contributions with an inscription in Hebrew, "*A gift in secret*" (Prov. xxi. 14).

Sometimes a mother belonging to one of the richer Oriental families puts on beggar's clothes and goes out barefoot to beg for the poor, in the hope that her alms-giving and self-abasement may avail with God to spare the life of her beloved child lying dangerously ill.

(3) *Riches.*—This subject has already been referred to in connection with the Trades. In the East the desire of gain is regarded as an instinct that imperatively seeks its own ends like hunger and thirst, and is common to humanity. A proverb says, "It is better to hear 'take' a thousand times than once the word 'give.'" The words of Christ, "It is better to give than to receive," were in such defiant contrast to common Oriental sentiment that they were remembered though unrecorded by the Evangelist (Acts xx. 35). The East has neither the eminent saints nor the great criminals of the West, but a dull air of avariciousness pervades every relationship. Marriage is a money-bargain ; murder has its equivalent price, piety is prudential, to go to a funeral is to *attend the merit*, and almsgiving is a current account with God.

8. Travel and Transport.—(1) *Oriental idea of travel.* —Among Orientals travel means discomfort, danger, and expense. It is avoided as much as possible. Their proverbs say, "All strangers are relatives to each other," "If three go on a journey, one must be elected chief," "A man in a strange place is blind though he has eye-sight," "There are three states of wretchedness—sickness, fasting, and travel." The following is the Oriental recipe or statute for one setting out upon a journey : "Pay all debts, provide for dependants, give parting gifts, return all articles under trust, take money and good temper for the journey ; then bid farewell to all, and be merciful to the animal you ride upon." In the East the road is usually a mere bridle path, rough and stony. When it passes along the side of their fields, the farmers empty the

stones upon it, as it belongs to nobody ; in the wilderness
it often forks off unexpectedly or disappears altogether.
In the long blank distances between the villages and
towns there is little chance of getting direction or help in
any difficulty. Something goes wrong with the harness,
a saddle-bag drops off noiselessly, the wrong path is taken,
or the distance is miscalculated and the night has to be
passed under the stars and without the needed water.
Orientals care little for beauty of scenery.   The wild
gorges and precipices belong to jackals and bats, and the
traveller cannot turn the trees into charcoal or carry the
sheaves to his own threshing-floor.   Travel for the enjoyment of the exercise and the pleasure of seeing new scenes
is a mystery to most of them.

The Bedawîn and peasants are often puzzled and
moved to laughter and pity when they see the companies
of English and American travellers who annually visit the
ancient sites of interest in the Holy Land.   Until they
come to understand the reason, their own surmise is that
they are searching for treasure in the ruins by means of
magic books, or visiting the shrines in order to atone for
their sins.

(2) *Mode of travel.*—Travelling is usually done by
riding, the animals being horses, mules, donkeys, and in
the sandy desert camels.   Summer is especially the time
for travel, as the rains are over, and the rivers can be
easily forded or crossed dry-shod.   Bridges are not
mentioned in the Bible.   The transport of goods and
merchandise is almost all done by baggage animals.
When muleteers are engaged to bring a certain number of
animals on an appointed day, it is customary to demand
a guarantee in money which is forfeited if they fail, and
returned if the contract be faithfully carried out.   In Jer.
xxx. 21, there is the beautiful figure of a *heart* given as a
pledge of good faith.   In the great waterless deserts

encountered in the journey to Palmyra, Baghdad, or Sinai,
camels are used, and the travelling is chiefly done by night
to escape the heat, and to escape the notice of the Bedawîn
tribes, whose neighbourhood is generally indicated by
lights or sounds of some sort.   Under such circumstances
the guide takes his direction from the stars.   In ancient
times the Bedawîn tribes were the great escorts of the
overland caravans.   During the time when they trans-
ported the treasures of the East to the Roman market
of the West, they became very rich and influential, and
founded under Zenobia the wonderful kingdom of Palmyra
or Tadmor.   The nation that does the trade of the world
by sea has now entered into their labours, and the Union
Jack in the Suez Canal takes the place of the camel's bell
in the star-led caravan.

(3) *Road-making.*—In different parts of the country
small pieces of the ancient Roman paved roads are still
seen as the memorial of work well done, but the ordinary roads of to-day are soon made almost impassable
by the rush of the winter rains.   When a distinguished
visitor arrives in the country, or the governor sets out on
a tour of inspection through his district, the roads are all
put into temporary repair by removing boulders and
filling up clefts and hollows, so that the passage over them
may be easy, quick, and safe.[1]

(4) *The forerunner.*—In the narrow streets of the
town thronged with men and baggage animals, high
officials have a servant in uniform walking in front of
them.   He calls out to the people to move aside, touches

---

[1] During the present summer several hundred men are engaged, by
order from Constantinople, on the roads leading from the coast to
Jerusalem and to the Sea of Galilee, preparing for the expected visit
of the Emperor of Germany in autumn.   When the occasion is over
the roads return to their usual Oriental condition.   Such preparations
are alluded to in Isaiah xl. 3-5.

with his rod the inattentive, stirs up the dogs lying in the path, and so clears the way for his master.   In Syria they are represented by the cavasses or guards of the consuls and the out-riders of the Pasha.   In Egypt two of them race in front of the carriage of the Khedive, and those of some of the principal native families have also one or two runners.

When the cry is heard all move aside instinctively, and in an instant there is the swift flutter of his white robes, the sparkle of a bright sash, a swing or two of the black tassel of the turban, then comes the carriage, and the cry of the forerunner is already sounding faint in the distance.

Being athletic young men specially selected and trained by constant exercise, they keep well in front of the carriage and its trotting horses, running along with the easy unspent lurch of a deer-hound.

Such was the cry raised in front of Joseph, the new vizier, long ago (Gen. xli. 43); thus Elijah raced in front of Ahab's chariot to Jezreel (1 Kings xviii. 46); and the office of the forerunner is especially associated with the name and work of John the Baptist (John i. 23).

(5) *Salutations.*—The formalities of Oriental salutation are chiefly derived from the dangers of travel.   It is the hail of approaching parties to know whether they are friends or foes (Josh. v. 13).   From the following epitome it will be seen how important was the command to the Gospel heralds to salute no man by the way.   Many other matters of compliment and courteous solicitude are introduced, and the same inquiries as to health, etc., are repeated over and over again.   As each must consider his own matters of no consequence compared with those of his friend, at the end of the salutation very little information is really obtained about either.

A. and B. are represented as meeting on the read.

A. Blessed is he that cometh.

B. And you twice blessed.

A. How is your health?

B. Well, by your favour.

A. By the favour of God.

B. God is merciful.

A. How is your work?

B. Praise be to God.

A. How is your father?

B. He sends you his salutation.

A. I have been longing to see him.

B. And he still more.

A. Can I do anything for you?

B. The Lord prolong your days.

A. That is a fine horse you have.

B. He would like to carry you.

A. When do you return, meaning no harm?

B. As the Lord wills.

A. The Lord be with you.

B. May you have peace.

The consideration of the labours, anxieties, and dangers incident to Oriental travel made the Israelites look back on the journey through the wilderness as a memorial and triumph of God's providence. It put the Queen of Sheba among those who have borne privation in the pursuit of knowledge (Matt. xii. 42). It gave depth and endearment of meaning to the "place of habitation" and the "city to dwell in." Oriental travel also helps us to understand, in its spiritual applications, what help is offered when our Lord calls Himself "the way," and what hope is held out with regard to welcome, rest, and blessedness, when life's pilgrimage leads at last to the City with open gates.

9. Medicine and Sickness.—The East has two names for its healers of disease, "the wise man" and "the holy man." In modern language this expresses the modern truth that medicine requires intelligence in the physician and the restfulness of trust on the part of the patient.

(1) *The wise man.*—Orientals have a great number of herbal remedies, but in their traditions the chief place is given to branding the flesh. They have not much faith in any one doctor, and call in one after another, and frequently summon consultations of doctors. It is a matter of family pride to have a large consultation, a gathering of eight or nine being quite common for a rich and important man. The experience of the woman mentioned in Mark v. 26 suggests that a similar custom prevailed in ancient times. The variety of treatment which the sufferer thus draws upon himself creates a wisdom that is supposed to be above that of the doctor, and gives rise to their proverbial saying, "Consult the patient, not the physician." The commonest ailments, apart from the effects of over-eating common to East and West, are ophthalmia, skin-disease, consumption, and fevers of the malarial and typhoidal types. The term applied to the sickness of Peter's mother-in-law (Luke iv. 38), "a strong fever," now describes a sharp attack of ague or malaria. It is not, of course, of an infectious character. Job seems to have suffered from the same trouble (Job xxx. 17-18), judging from the symptoms of aching bones and fever sweat.

(2) *The holy man.*—The religious or superstitious view of healing regards health as the natural condition, and disease the departure to be accounted for. God is on the side of life and has power over permitted sickness, but commits this power only to those who commit themselves to Him. This is the point at which in Oriental custom truth departs and imposture enters. The reputation for sainthood is obtained by fasting, pilgrimage, magic books, and attention to the forms of religion. In

riding through the land one sometimes sees far up on a
lonely but conspicuous cliff a rude contrivance of poles
and leaves, and learns on inquiry that a man is spending
his days and nights there, living upon the bread and
water brought to him, giving his whole time to prayer,

AMULET.

and so accumulating the merit and holiness that in course
of time will bring to him inquirers with suitable presents.

The Christian saints, Moslem dervishes, and Jewish
chachams, who heal by religious power, appeal to the
superstitious veneration of the people, and, with all
their absurd and often disgusting orders, they show a
shrewd knowledge of how the troubled heart can be
comforted, and the will may receive a new determination
to live and not die. Their help is chiefly appealed to in

cases that have the appearance of Satanic possession, such as insanity, epilepsy, and estranged affection.

The first preaching of the Gospel in Samaria, Cyprus, Philippi, Ephesus, and other places, encountered opposition from such holy men and their vested interests. The ceremony of exorcism is still practised, chiefly among the uneducated Moslems, and the process and result are described by them with much confidence and in full detail. The good-humoured smile of the European doctor is its worst enemy. Associated with this form of treatment is the popular and almost universal device of wearing amulets of some sort to guard against the evil eye and Satanic influences.

Among the Jews the chief protective symbol is the phylactery, a small black box about a cubic inch in size, containing Ex. xiii. 5-9 ; Deut. vi. 4-9, xi. 13-21. At prayer on week-days one is fastened on the brow and another on the left arm by the leather straps attached to them. The Pharisees made these boxes large and the straps broad, Matt. xxiii. 5.

In the case of Asa (2 Chr. xvi. 12), who consulted the physicians instead of entreating the Lord for recovery, we should not understand that a contrast is implied between faith - healing and physical remedies. Those Oriental physicians would also appeal to supernatural influences ; but, like the rabbis of the present day, it would be to angels or demons whose names are too mighty and sacred to be pronounced, such as Senoi, Sansenoi, and Samnan-galeph. To accept the great science of medicine as a gift from God is at once the largest exercise of religious feeling and of reason.

Orientals show the value they attach to faith by the often quoted proverb, "Have faith, though it be only in a stone, and you will recover."

The tendency to superstition is seen in another maxim

which resembles one of the so-called *Sayings of Christ* recently discovered in Egypt, namely, "The church that is close at hand can work no cures."[1]

The deep-laid conviction that while the use of means is a human duty, the healing is a work of Divine power, survives the ancient impostures that have been heaped upon it, and at the present day gives special appropriateness and influence to the medical missionary in all Oriental lands.

10. Education.—Oriental education is especially in the interests of religious knowledge and morality. The school is an appendage to the church, mosque, or synagogue. Its importance is indicated by the proverb: "The teaching of children is like engraving in stone, the teaching of adults like waves on the sea." Children are sent to school almost in infancy, and remain till the twelfth or thirteenth year. The Oriental theory of instruction includes the influences of both education and heredity. "You can only take out of a pot what you put into it," and, "If the father be onion and the mother garlic, how can there be any sweet perfume?"

The teaching is chiefly done by making the children recite sentences and passages after the teacher. His ambition is that the clamour of the voices chanting in concert may be well heard by those who pass by in the street. It proves to the parents that work is being done, and brings other children to his school. The school among the Jews is called "the house of the book"—that is the Bible, especially the Pentateuch. In the reading of the Bible and the Jewish Prayer-book a knowledge of manuscript Hebrew writing is also taught, having different characters for the Askenazim or European Jews and the Sepharidim or Oriental Jews. This Hebrew script is used

---

[1] "Jesus saith, 'A prophet is not acceptable in his own country, neither doth a physician work cures upon them that know him.'"

in letter-writing and book-keeping whatever may be the language that is used—English, Arabic, Russian, German, or Sanscrit.

Next in importance to the rules of religion is the teaching of languages as a means of social contact and commercial success. Education as a mental discipline is not understood.

Popular literature is represented by the crowds sitting in the café in the evenings and listening to the story-teller reciting tales of demon influence, war exploits, and discovered treasure, such as abound in the *Arabian Nights*. A favourite study among the more thoughtful is found in proverbial literature. The Book of Proverbs is prized by Jews, Christians, and Moslems alike.

The Arabs have a vast stock of proverbial sayings gleaned from the whole field of nature and experience. Great and guiding thoughts of the wise are expressed in forms of much force and beauty, though the emphasis often goes far beyond the requirements of plain fact. This exaggeration is an onslaught on the door of Truth in order to awaken the porter Judgment who lies asleep within. The rhymed poetical form in which most of the Proverbs are cast makes them easily remembered and keeps them in constant use. Many of them show great acuteness in the detection of a resembling point between things that differ in kind. The beautiful and persuasive parables of Christ appealed to this enjoyment and appreciation of similitudes among Orientals.

11. Religion. —Religion is the great fact of Oriental life.

" Of Him, and through Him, and to Him are all things " (Rom. xi. 36), such is the acclamation of everything that lives or has a name to live in the East.

Christianity, Judaism, and Islam have many deep distinctions, but they are all one with regard to the existence and power of God. In the East, to be without religion is not an intellectual view but a moral void. Scepticism is still regarded as the self-defence of a disobedient heart (Ps. **xiv.** 1). To deny and to prove the existence of God are considered almost equally frivolous.

So strong and universal is this conviction with regard to the glory of God's name, that if the Missionary Gospel could only find an entrance into the mind and heart, and cause love to be added to faith, the East might again send forth a wave of religious influence that would carry blessing to the world.

Oriental religion has a heart of profound reverence, but it is almost paralysed by superstition, fatalism, and formality.

A. *Superstition.*—In the multiplying of mediators between God and man, Oriental Christianity has fallen into an error from which Judaism and Islam are comparatively free. Faith in amulets is, however, common to all, and the power of the evil eye and the discovery of secret things by means of witchcraft are widespread superstitions. The revealer of secrets by necromancy or communication with the dead is called in Arabic *a seer.* This name and practice go back to the days of Samuel. In 1 Sam. ix. 7 an embarrassment arises about consulting the man of God without having a present to give him. The word translated "present" means in Hebrew and Arabic *a direction fee,* and the creation of this technical term implies that such appeals to the seer were popular and had a recognised commercial value. Another similarity that shows the continuity of these dark traditions is that the Hebrew name for a wizard, "*one who knows,*" is in the living Arabic of to-day "*one who tells.*" Again, when the Bible speaks of a man or woman with *a familiar spirit,* the term means *one who makes use of a bottle.* This is explained by the modern practice in the East. If a sum of money disappears in a house, the witch who is summoned to reveal where it is hidden and by whom it has been stolen always brings an empty bottle with her. By this medium she professes to appeal to the dead relatives of the party who has lost the money, and the audible answers are declared to proceed from the bottle.

B. *Fatalism.*—The doctrine of fate is constantly resorted to, not only in submitting to the inevitable, but in excusing carelessness and indolence. Personal disposition cannot, and public custom must not be changed. The Jew fulfils all righteousness in following Jewish traditions, and so with the Christian and Moslem. All admit that the supreme end of religion is to glorify God, but the way to that end is rutted and blocked by the transport waggons of ceremonial and legal ordinance. Israel has *the certainty of the commandments,* and to this Islam adds *the duty of submission,* but only the Gospel of *the grace of God* can change the outward law into inward preference, and self-surrender into perfect freedom. It is the hope and prayer of the Christian Church, which sends its missionaries to labour in Syria and Palestine, that the Holy Spirit may speedily bless the means used towards the accomplishment of this great result. God has not cast off His ancient people, it is not His will that Ishmael should perish, nor is it in vain that the Christian name has been preserved through centuries of trial and oppression. There is blessing in store for the land in which "the Word was made flesh and dwelt among us."

Even now the religious thought of the East teaches a lesson that is often greatly needed in more enlightened lands. Those who have handed down so much of the outward form from ancient times have also preserved this inward truth, that the mission of religion is not so much to satisfy the highest claims of the intellect as to supply the deepest needs of the heart. In the West, God does a certain thing because He is good ; in the East, the same

thing is good because He has done it.   God is greater
than East and West, but these have much to learn from
each other.   The East shrinks from prescribing what God
must do.   There may be fatalism in definitions as well as
in destiny.   It is hard to enclose the purpose of eternity
in the formula of a day.   The religion that has for its
first truth and its terminus *"the name of Jesus,"* will
constantly find its system of theology thrown out of
perspective by the changing face and new proportions of
an ever-expanding Ideal.

C. *Formality.*—While this abounds in the Oriental
Church as well as in the Synagogue, its illustration in the
latter presents details of greater interest on account of the
connection with Bible history, and because it shows what
things are preferred to the still rejected Gospel of the
Lord Jesus Christ.

The life of a Jew is religious from the cradle to the
grave.   In the room occupied by the mother and her new-
born infant the rabbi puts a paper containing Ps. cxxi. in
Hebrew, with an intercession for the favour of Adam and
Eve and the good angels, and an anathema against the
power or approach of Leilith, the demon of the night.

After completing his thirteenth year a Jewish boy is
taken by his father to the synagogue, and there made "a
son of the Commandment."   The father thanks God for
release from moral responsibility over the boy's actions, as
he has now received the spirit of discernment between
good and evil (comp. Phil. i. 9, 10).   When the Jew rises
in the morning he puts on under his vest the small
tallith or prayer-cloth with its sacred fringes, and goes
through the prescribed morning devotions in the house or
synagogue.

There are set and separate *graces* in Hebrew to be said
in connection with bread, meat, wine, and fruit.   Those for
scents are specialised as adapted to bark, blossoms, leaves,

or fragrant powder. There are similar phrases for the sight
of anything beautiful or wonderful in nature, for hearing
a word of wisdom, or meeting a man eminent in piety.
These are all learnt by heart in childhood, in a language
that is not used for common conversation and daily life.

In the house, on the right-hand door-post of each
inhabited room, there is the *mezûza*, a small box containing
the commandment in Deut. vi. 4-9. The custom may at
one time have had a beautiful significance as a reminder
of the unseen Guest in the house Whose presence should
control and hallow all that is said and done in it, but it is
now merely an amulet or charm protecting the sleepers
against the entrance of any demons of the night.   Outside
of the house there are the synagogue prayers for morning,
afternoon, and evening, with special additions for the
weekly Sabbath and the religious Festivals.   The service
of God is always presented as a law that has to be
carried out both in its evident meanings and in the far-
fetched and often facetious inferences drawn from them.
Rabbinical teaching resembles a statute on copyright or
the game-laws.   Thus, with regard to the sin of seething
a kid in its mother's milk (Ex. xxiii. 29) : (1) The dish is
utterly prohibited ; (2) to guard against the accidental
mingling of the two things, the same vessel must not be
used for milk and meat ; (3) an interval must be allowed
between the eating of meat and milk ; (4) if the former
be eaten first, the interval must be longer, as it takes
longer to digest ; (5) curded milk must be classified as
meat because it contains rennet.   To trace such filigree
inferences from a hypothetical case is, rabbinically, to
deepen the spiritual life.   It is profoundly natural that
after such rules are all carried out a loving heart should
say, " What lack I yet ? " (Matt. xix. 20).

Apart from the regulations about special matters and
the weekly Sabbath, the religious life of the Jews is

controlled by the round of the sacred Festivals, and can be best illustrated by a brief description of them and the manner of their observance. At every turn we shall have to notice how "the letter killeth," but as we do so, let us remember that the same loveless formality which has brought this blight on the natural branches may do as much or more to the engrafted.

There are eight principal Festivals, of which five have their origin in the Pentateuch.[1]

(1) *Passover*, Ex. xii. 1-28, from the 15th to the end of the 21st of lunar April (Abîb or Nisân).—This is a time of great preparation and rejoicing in the Jewish families. It is the beginning of the religious year. When the sun sets on the 14th day and the stars begin to appear, everything is in readiness for the celebration. The great house-cleaning is over, the members of the family are dressed in new clothes, and through the fastened doors and windows in the Jewish quarter of the town one hears on every side the high nasal swing of many voices reading Hebrew in concert. The Samaritans alone keep up the custom of roasting lambs according to the original directions, but all have the bitter herbs, chiefly dandelion leaves, and the mortar-like sauce with which they are eaten in remembrance of the bondage in Egypt. During the reading the head of the family explains the circumstances commemorated, and asks each of the young sons present where he is going, and receives the answer, "I am going from the land of Egypt to the land of Jerusalem." This form is used

---

[1] It will be remembered that the Jews observe the lunar year, which being shorter than the solar, causes the dates to move forward until they are checked and brought back to solar time by the insertion of an extra twelfth month, Adar; that the lunar month does not always begin on the same day as that of the solar year, and usually includes days from two different months according to the Western reckoning, and that the Jewish day always begins with the sunset of the previous evening (Gen. i. 5).

because the names Mizrâim and Yerushalâim (Egypt and Jerusalem) form a rhyme. Four cups of wine are appointed to be drunk during the celebration. For obvious reasons of comfort and decorum the wine is diluted with water. It must be of the best quality obtainable, and free from Gentile contamination. The poor may use raisin-water.

During the time of preparation great care is taken to rid the house of leaven and leavened bread, and every utensil used for making, holding, or carrying it. When the house has been thoroughly searched and cleansed by the women, the master makes his official and solemn search. As he does so in the name of God, a piece of bread is laid in a conspicuous place, as, if he found nothing, it would be like taking God's name in vain! Sometimes a man is engaged to make a nominal purchase of everything fermented in the house or that might become so, such as vinegar, wine, syrup, and preserved fruits. He asks to have them left there till he calls for them. He calls after the seven days of the Passover feast are over and gives them back for the same sum. During the interval the articles in question did not belong, rabbinically, to the family! In making the unleavened bread, the modern Pharisee has a piece of muslin put over the mouth of the jar in which the water is brought from the fountain in case a crumb of common bread might accidentally float into the vessel. Nothing is ever said in the spirit of 1 Cor. v. 8.

(2) *Pentecost.*—This occurs fifty days after the beginning of Passover, on the 7th lunar day of June (Sivân). It is also called the Feast of Harvest (Ex. xxiii. 16), and the Feast of Weeks (Deut. xvi. 6). In the synagogue the appointment of the seventy elders is commemorated (Ex. xxiv. 1 ; Num. xi. 16).

(3) *The ninth of August* (Ab).—This is kept in remembrance as the dark day on which the first and second

Temples were destroyed and Jerusalem was ploughed over. The synagogue furniture is overthrown and littered about, the worshippers fast, and have their clothes soiled and disordered, the Book of Lamentations is read, and prayer is offered for the coming of the promised Deliverer.

(4) *The Feast of Trumpets* (Lev. xxiii. 24 ; Num. xxix.) —This, the 1st of October (Ethanim or Tisri) is the beginning of the secular year.   It acquires religious importance as the first of the *ten days of repentance* before the Day of Atonement.   Tradition teaches that on this New Year's day the names of those Israelites who are to die during the current year are written down in the Book of Death, and the names of those who are to survive it in the Book of Life.

The opportunity afforded by the ten days is that of having the name possibly transferred from one book to the other by means of increased attention to prayer, penance, and the rules and claims of the synagogue. This superstition is superior to that of the Roman Catholic Confessional and Mass, inasmuch as the decision rests with God and not with the priest, but it serves the same purpose of moral intimidation and mercenary pressure, and represents blessing as laboriously wrung from God.

(5) *Day of Atonement* (Lev. xvi. 3-10; Num. xxix. 7-11). —This day, 10th October, is one of special solemnity.   Jews who absent themselves from the synagogue during the rest of the year are present and take part in the all-day service. White cocks and hens are killed as symbolical of forgiveness and purity.   White clothes are worn for the same reason, and the whole day is spent in reciting prayers of humiliation and penitence.   The vehement gestures and voices choked with sobs make the stranger feel that he is looking upon the anguish of some great bereavement.   It is like a soul trying to recover a lost instinct or re-enter some previous state of existence.   It is the annual pageant

of penitence, but it is powerless to change the heart (Heb. x. 3, 4).

(6) *The Feast of Tabernacles* (Lev. xxiii. 34; Num. xxix. 12; Deut. xvi. 30).—This begins after sunset on the 14th of October. It was the harvest home or thanksgiving day for the ingathering of the fruits of the summer, especially raisins, figs, and olives. During the eight days of this feast the Jews erect tabernacles or arbours of branches and calico awnings on the balconies and flat roofs of their houses and take their meals there.

(7) *The Feast of Lights*, 25th December (Chisleu), John x. 22, commemorates the restoration of the Temple service after the sacred place had been desecrated in the time of the Maccabees by Antiochus Epiphanes, B.C. 168-165.

(8) *The Feast of Purim* (Est. ix. 19) is held on the 14th of March (Adar). The roll of the Book of Esther is read through in the synagogue, the name of Mordecai being hailed with blessings and that of Haman with imprecations. It is the Gunpowder-plot Day of Jewish history with Haman as conspirator. His effigy is made and pelted by the children, and the rich send gifts of food to the poor so that all Israel may rejoice. It is customary to say of a well-furnished table or a hearty meal that it is a *feast of Purim*.

The synagogue service and festivals are chiefly valued by the Jews as a means, the only one left to them, of declaring and preserving their distinction as a race. They become the substitute rather than the support of true religious feeling, as every commemoration of the past finds its contradiction in the facts of present-day circumstance. Thus Passover recalls the fact of the national name and place to those who have neither. The agricultural feasts of Pentecost and Tabernacles are celebrated by those who shrink from manual labour. The Jew is proverbially the emigrant and wanderer of the earth, but he daily recites in his Prayer-book, "Lord, I thank Thee that Thou hast not made me a foreigner."

It is a strange anomaly that the national bond of union should be found in those very formalities that emphasise the fact of the people's severance from their original conditions. There is much in these particulars that should appeal pathetically to the sympathy of the Christian who knows that what is needed is God's gift of pardon and righteousness and the constraining love of Christ.

Perhaps the crowning instance of such contradiction between the past and the present is seen at the close of the synagogue service, when the priest's face is veiled with the tallith as he pronounces the benediction of Moses (Num. vi. 24-26). This precaution is observed lest the utterance of the words of Moses by one occupying his place should bring up the glory that shone upon the face of the great lawgiver, and so strike the people dead.

This tyranny of empty form and the limiting to one nation of what God has thrown open to the whole world give to the Christian Church its missionary duty towards Israel. It is the message of the younger brother who once wasted his substance to the elder who is now in danger of being impoverished by his. This exclusive claim to God's favour was and remains the line of cleavage between the synagogue and the church. It is zeal, but not according to knowledge; for the truth which the Jews reject is that God's glory is exhibited in the saving of all nations (Acts ii. 21-39, iii. 25, vi. 14, x. 28-43, xiii. 47, xiv. 27, xvii. 27, xxii. 21, 22; 1 Tim. ii. 7).

Palestine is a land of sacred memories. Some of them still retain the tones of the living voice, while others are bleached and faded inscriptions recording on the tombstone what was done when the breath of life was warm.

The great truth of personal religion which the East during

the centuries has taught by symbol and sacrifice, and often debased by formality and superstition, is that God entrusts His power to those who entrust themselves to Him.   The story of its institutions and their expansion from primitive times is an unfolding of the great social law that the individual exists for the family, the family for the nation, the nation for the world, and the world for God.

With regard to the Bible itself this study of Manners and Customs has set before us a great array of surviving thoughts, habits, and institutions that explain and confirm the allusions to similar details in the Bible.   It has shown us how fully and familiarly the message of revelation was adapted to human circumstances.

The impression thus left upon the mind is that the Bible is a book that is meant to be studied, and to be taken on its merits as a record of the past, and above all that it is to be loved and reverenced as the voice of Him who through it speaks for ever, and to all nations.

INDEX OF SUBJECTS

INDEX OF TEXTS